SWANSEA CITY
MATCH
OF MY LIFE

CHRIS CARRA

First published by Pitch Publishing, 2018

Pitch Publishing
A2 Yeoman Gate
Yeoman Way
Worthing
Sussex
BN13 3QZ
www.pitchpublishing.co.uk
info@pitchpublishing.co.uk

ISBN 978-1-78531-424-7

Typesetting and origination by Pitch Publishing

Printed and bound in India by Replika Press Pvt. Ltd.

SWANSEA CITY
MATCH
OF MY LIFE

Contents

Acknowledgements 7

Introduction 9

Foreword 12

Mel Nurse
Swansea Town 6-1 Leicester City 17

Vic Gomersall
Swansea Town 0-1 Arsenal 29

David Gwyther
Oxford City 1-5 Swansea Town 41

John Toshack
Preston North End 1-3 Swansea City 51

Alan Curtis
Swansea City 5-1 Leeds United 59

Leighton James
Liverpool 2-2 Swansea City 69

Wyndham Evans
Swansea City 0-0 Manchester United 81

John Cornforth
Swansea City 1-1 Huddersfield Town 93

Michael Howard
Swansea City 2-1 Cardiff City 105

Roger Freestone
Swansea City 1-0 West Ham United 117

Matthew Bound
Rotherham United 1-1 Swansea City 129

James Thomas
Swansea City 4-2 Hull City 141

Lee Trundle
Swansea City 2-1 Carlisle United 153

Alan Tate
Reading 2-4 Swansea City 163

Nathan Dyer
Swansea City 5-0 Bradford City 175

Leon Britton
Swansea City 3-0 Cardiff City 183

Dedication

To my parents – Helen and Antonio
– for their hard work and constant support.

Acknowledgements

THIS is my third book, and it never becomes any more of a solo venture. In fact, this book has relied more on other people than the past two combined. I therefore have a hefty list of acknowledgements.

Naturally, I'm indebted to the 16 Swansea City legends who willingly gave up their time, with no financial reward, to share their wonderful stories with me. In the order that I interviewed them, a massive thank you to: Mel Nurse, Leighton James, Alan Curtis, Wyndham Evans, Roger Freestone, Alan Tate, Vic Gomersall, John Toshack, Matthew Bound, James Thomas, Dai Gwyther, Michael Howard, Lee Trundle, John Cornforth, Leon Britton and Nathan Dyer.

To that list you can also add John Hartson, for agreeing to write the superb foreword. He's a diehard Swans fan and a lovely guy. I just wish he had played for the Swans – I would have had another brilliant chapter on my hands!

I'm also hugely grateful to those who helped put me in touch with the players I interviewed. The media team at Swansea City – Jonathan Wilsher, Gareth Vincent and Chris Barney – were very helpful, while I also exhausted both Ian and Alan Curtis with several other requests (of which they always happily obliged).

On that note, a big thank you to Mark Rees, Alec Johnson and Cameron Toshack for helping me get hold of other key players. Mat Davies at the *Evening Post* was also very helpful with both contacts and photos, while I thank Jonathan Roberts and Tony Woolway for their cooperation with the photos too. If I've forgotten anyone, I'm very sorry!

Without everyone at Pitch Publishing, this book wouldn't exist – in terms of putting together a quality product and trusting me with such an ambitious project in the first place. For that, I thank Paul and Jane Camillin, and Graham Hales, as well as fellow author Nick Johnson for his early advice.

Three good friends – Robert Dalling, Joe Tobin and Steven Hirst – put up with my nagging and pretty much read the entire book between them as chapters were finished, giving me great feedback on first drafts. Thanks guys!

I'm also going to take this opportunity to thank everyone who has continued to support myself and my books – this one and the previous two. It's hugely appreciated.

Of course, I am hugely grateful to my parents and to all my family for their constant support. This is extended to my friends – while they may not have contributed to the book directly, they usually gave me a reason to ditch the computer for a coffee/beer. In particular Daniel Francis, Richard Perdue, Daniel Oakes and Steve Homer, as well as anyone who shared a session of Titan Conditioning with me.

My final and biggest thanks go to my girlfriend Becci, who continues to put up with my general insanity, as she has done with great patience for the past 13 years.

Introduction

YOU hold in your hands the result of months of hard work, plenty of swearing, and endless cups of coffee.

And it was totally worth it.

Based on a series of exclusive interviews, 16 legends of Swansea City Football Club recall their favourite match in a Swans shirt – the build-up, the nerves, the fights, the goals and the glory of games that have shaped the club and the city as a whole.

I started writing this book in June 2017. Despite the success of my previous two books, this time I wanted to go big. I decided to tackle one of the more ambitious titles in Pitch Publishing's huge collection, *Match of My Life*.

Unlike the past two, this book saw me forced out of my computer-based comfort zone and into the world of actually meeting people for a chat. Back to the good old days then.

As I began the journey, the biggest question was 'Could I get the players on board?' There was only one way to find out.

Although I made a rough shortlist of those players I wanted to chat to, I always knew I was going to start with Mel Nurse – probably because he seemed one of the most approachable, usually visible in the window of his guesthouse overlooking Swansea Bay.

Anyone who has been lucky enough to speak with Mel before will know how dedicated he is to Swansea – the city and the football club. If Mel didn't want to take part, I knew the book wouldn't get off the ground.

Thankfully he was only too happy to chat with me about his time with the Swans and his debut match in 1956. His anecdotes and stories made for an excellent chapter, offering a true taste of what life was like growing up and playing professional football in the 1950s.

One down, 15 to go.

Rather than just settling with anyone who said yes (although, when my leads occasionally dried up, that started to seem like a good plan), I wanted the book to reflect a balance of the past 60 or so years of the club's history.

So, I invited a few of the older former players to contribute their stories. I had very pleasant meetings with Dai Gwyther and Vic Gomersall, who both had great stories to tell. Both were very enthusiastic about this book, and Vic even came to our initial meeting armed with rare original newspaper clippings from his favourite match. Even better, he invited me to his home a few weeks later where we edited his chapter together.

What surprised me was how happy each player was to contribute. These men, who are still very busy with their own lives, gave up their time to have a chat with me. They didn't complain when I fussed around with the batteries for my voice recorder, or when I rang them out of the blue – sometimes more than once – to clarify something I had forgotten to ask.

It was such a pleasure to meet the stars of the 1980s First Division success – Alan Curtis, Leighton James and Wyndham Evans – not to mention the man who masterminded it all, John Toshack. These men were icons at the time and are still fondly remembered by all Swans fans. It was an honour to meet and speak with them about their days at the club.

Another player I really enjoyed chatting to was John Cornforth, who currently lives in Sunderland. While I was unable to meet him face-to-face, I had a few nice phone conversations with the memorable captain, who turned out to be one of the funniest players I interviewed.

In August, I went to the Liberty Stadium to watch Alan Tate's deserved testimonial match. The following day I drove to Newport to meet Roger Freestone at his home. The legendary goalkeeper was still aching all over following a fantastic airing the previous evening, but his pain was worth it for Swans fans to once again witness some of those dramatic saves!

Over the months, I was also able to meet with some players who made a big impact on Swansea around the turn of the century. I spoke with Matthew Bound at his office in Mumbles, while I shared coffee with Michael Howard, Lee Trundle, and hat-trick hero James Thomas in central Swansea.

I was also lucky enough to meet Alan Tate at the club's training ground in Landore on a glorious summer's day – a pleasure to see the top-class facilities the club utilise and a bigger pleasure to spend some time with one of my personal favourite players. The same goes for chatting with both Leon Britton and Nathan Dyer at the Swans' Fairwood base as I approached the end of the book.

As smoothly as much of it went, this project was not without a few little setbacks.

There were a couple of other players I was keen to get on board, but – for one reason or another – it never happened.

Despite a long chase, a stalwart of the 1960s simply wasn't interested in contributing his story, having gone off football in recent years – we had a nice chat over the phone about his time with the Swans, although he couldn't be persuaded.

I was a little annoyed with myself after speaking with a modern-day legend, who agreed to contribute a chapter. However, as it was such a fleeting encounter, I forgot to get his details. He lives abroad now and I wasn't able to track him down again.

I also made contact with a few others but couldn't pin them down for a proper chat, and eventually conceded that it wasn't going to happen. Either that or I simply ran out of time.

One of my favourite things about the book is that each chapter has a different dynamic. If you're expecting minute-by-minute match reports from the players, you'll be disappointed. Of course, some players had excellent memories of the on-field action, whereas others preferred to use the match of their lives as a focal point to talk about their careers with Swansea.

But it's more interesting to hear the dressing room banter, the big-match preparation, and what the celebrations were like from the people who experienced it first-hand. It's the stuff football fans don't usually see, which makes it more special.

Naturally, the majority of games selected were wins, although there were a few draws and one brave defeat. We have both league and cup matches; matches home and away; matches at the Vetch and the Liberty Stadium; a handful of Wembley visits and a few South Wales derby matches.

Ultimately, it's been one of the most enjoyable projects I've ever worked on. I'm incredibly proud. It wasn't always easy, but the best books rarely are.

So, to the players who contributed to this historic collection, I really hope I've done justice to your fantastic stories.

And to the reader, I sincerely hope you enjoy.

Chris Carra

Note: The games and goals stats used at the beginning of every chapter signifies league games and league goals only. Some figures were difficult to accurately determine, but these offer a general guide.

Foreword

John Hartson

Sunday, 28 January 2018

IT'S AN honour to have been asked to write the foreword for this book, which is a cracking collection of some of the club's biggest legends sharing their personal stories of their favourite matches.

Ever since I was a little boy, I've been the biggest Swansea City supporter.

My earliest memories were going down to the Vetch with my dad and sitting on his shoulders in the old North Bank, which I absolutely loved. You had the steel bars separating the rows that I used to sit on too, with my dad standing behind me to make sure I didn't fall off!

The North Bank always used to be jam-packed and swaying as one. Over to my right you would have the chanters and singers, around 300 of them pointing and singing at the away end – sometimes they would be trying to get over the fence and into that end!

When I got to around 14 years old, I was playing for teams like Lonlas Boys' Club and Winch Wen on a Saturday. We would kick off at half two and, being youngsters, we would only play 30 minutes each way. Then we'd all pile in the back of my father's van, he'd drive us down to the Vetch and we would all go in to watch the second half of the Swans match.

As I got older again, I started my own football career. I left home at the age of around 16, but whenever I was injured, or whenever I had a suspension – and I had one or two of those over the years! – I would come back home to watch the Swans. It was around £4.50 to get in back then, and I would go and sit in the stands with the other Jacks.

This was Swansea in the old Third and Fourth Division. The highest-paid player would have been on around £600 a week, and sometimes the crowds were as low as 3,500. But I still got the same enjoyment then as I do now, because – to me – it was my club, and it was somewhere I was always going to go.

I think that stemmed from a very early age, as my father was a big Swans fan, as were the whole family, and I don't think that ever leaves you.

I went on to play for eight clubs; some of the biggest teams in Great Britain – the likes of Arsenal, West Ham and Celtic. But all the while there's only ever been one team for me, and that's Swansea City.

As I first went to watch the club I can vaguely remember players like Alan Curtis, Nigel Stevenson, Jeremy Charles and Dai Davies playing for us. I can remember those were the days of the Swan on the shirt and tight, tight shorts. I'm not sure I could have ever fitted into those shorts in my playing days!

But the team of my era was certainly late 1980s and early 90s. I always remember the likes of Tommy Hutchinson, Chris Coleman, Paul Raynor, David D'Auria, and Jan Molby. We weren't making history on the pitch, but it was a good team to watch.

Of course, growing up, it was an ambition of mine to play for Swansea, but it was never made to happen. This was because – and no disrespect to the club – when Swansea were playing in the Third and Fourth Division, I was banging in goals for Arsenal and West Ham in the Premier League.

When I was getting a bit older – a bit heavier in my shorts, if you like – the biggest opportunity to join Swansea presented itself.

There were serious conversations at one stage. It was around 2007 when I had a meeting with Roberto Martinez, Huw Jenkins and Martin Morgan. We sat around a table in Morgan's Hotel and nearly got it done. I nearly, nearly signed for Swansea City.

But nothing materialised in the end. At the time Swansea were going well, and were on the way to winning the league, back when Roberto had them playing great football. Attacking-wise they already had Andy Robinson and Lee Trundle, with Ferrie Bodde behind them, so they had plenty of talent in that sense.

To this day I have no real regrets that it didn't happen. I had a great career and, like coming through cancer, I played the hand that I was dealt. Let's just say that it was a disappointment not to play for the Swans, although I don't lie in bed awake at night worrying about it.

However, as a footballer, you do dread the day you play against your home club and, for me, that day came in January 1999, in the FA Cup third round. Reading Roger Freestone's chapter in this book brings back some memories of a very tough game.

It was really hard to play against the Swans that day, being such a big supporter and with the Swans fans singing my name. Don't get me wrong, if I had the chance to score, I would have scored, but it didn't make it any easier.

It was a difficult match when Swansea came to West Ham, but Julian Dicks scored a long-range effort in the last minute to equalise and force the replay.

We actually came down to Swansea three days before the replay to prepare. Harry Redknapp loved Swansea, and he took us to the beaches and for walks along Mumbles. We had a cracking build-up, with my friends and family coming down to the hotel to visit me. It was great.

But we got completely turned over on the night! Swansea really got in our faces, and they weren't in fear of the big names. We had Ruddock, Dicks, Cole, Ferdinand, Lampard, Kitson and myself – all senior Premier League players.

It was a windy, rainy, swirly sort of night, and there wasn't a free seat in the house – the Vetch was bouncing. That atmosphere was amplified as soon as Martin Thomas's 20-yard winner flew in.

There were no excuses from us though. I didn't play particularly well, and as a team we didn't turn up. Swansea were the opposite – right up for it and they deserved the result.

Oddly, I didn't know it at the time, but that would be my last match for West Ham.

I never really got to grieve about the result with my team-mates because, out of the blue, I was sold the next day.

I always remember on the bus on the way back to London, Harry Redknapp sat next to me all the way home. We talked about life, my family, my parents, what school I went to – everything.

The next morning, we had a day off, so I went for a game of golf. I was putting out on the fifth hole and the club pro turned up on his buggy.

'Is John Hartson part of your team?' he asked.

'Yeah, here I am,' I said.

'We've had a phone call. You need to get to this address in the centre of London, to meet Sam Hammam and Joe Kinnear.'

I signed for Wimbledon the very next morning.

Harry Redknapp had sat next to me for four hours, got to know me, then sold me the next day. It was very strange. Regardless, I went for £7.5m, which would have been £72m, in today's money.

So, I had broken the Arsenal transfer record, I had broken the West Ham transfer record, and now I had smashed the Wimbledon transfer record.

Going back to Swans, this book is full of legendary names, including John Toshack, who is my hero. What he did for Swansea is remarkable, a real one-off. I can't speak highly enough of him – he's a top manager with an amazing CV, and an all-round great man.

You've also got other club legends such as Mel Nurse (even though his 'Match of My Life' was a bit before my time!), John Cornforth and Alan Curtis.

I enjoyed Alan Tate's story of the Championship play-off final in 2011, when Swansea finally made it into the Premier League in front of 40,000

Swans fans. I was at Wembley with my son for that match and it was genuinely like a home game – bumping into old friends and people that we knew from Swansea.

I remember we were 3-0 up at half-time and we had gone down for a cup of tea in the break. As we were coming back up the steps a little into the second half it was 3-2. Bloody hell, we had missed two Reading goals! We sat anxiously for another 20 minutes, then Scotty Sinclair had his penalty, completed his hat-trick, and we ended up winning 4-2.

As the final whistle went, you realise – after all the players, all the managers and all those years, we had finally made it into the Premier League. Just like Tatey, we sat at Wembley for two hours after everyone else had left, just taking it all in.

In the last ten years or so, we have been spoiled as Swans fans. I'm the biggest Swans fan out there and can admit that.

We've seen promotions, we've been to Wembley several times, we've won the League Cup, and played in Europe. We've had some really good managers that have always been able to take us forward.

In the last two years we've spent a lot of time at the bottom of the table, but we were always going to hit a wall. The last decade has been such a high, naturally our luck would even itself out.

As I write this foreword, Swansea are fighting for survival in the Premier League table, and we seem to have lost our way a little bit, both on and off the pitch.

I can't predict exactly where we'll be when this book is published, but I know that whatever happens, the Jack Army – myself included – will always be there, a force to be reckoned with.

Once again, I'm honoured to be part of this excellent book, and I hope you enjoy it.

John Hartson

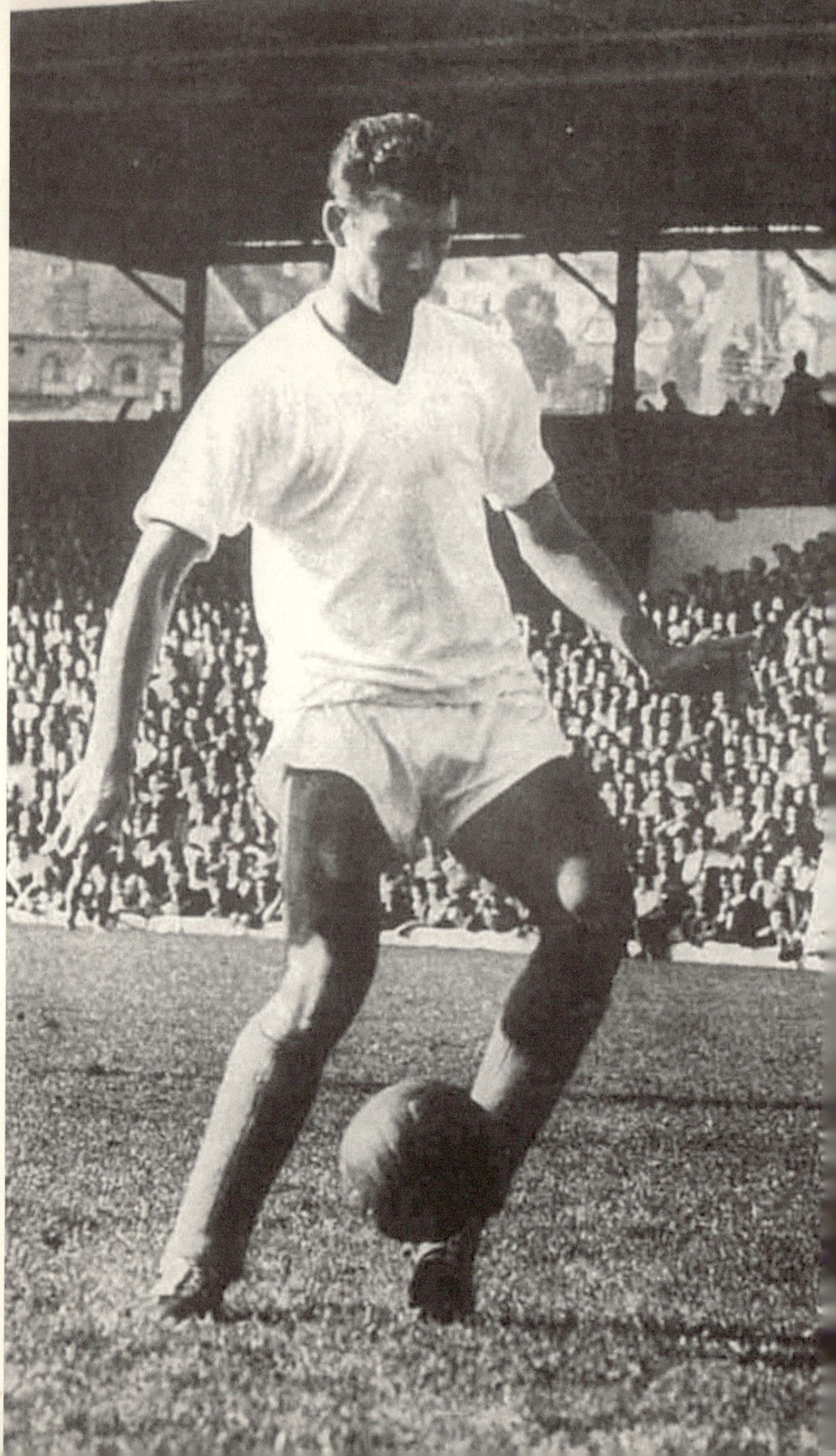

MEL NURSE: BORN 11 OCTOBER 1937, SWANSEA; 257 GAMES, 12 GOALS

Mel Nurse

Swansea Town 6-1 Leicester City
Football League Second Division
The Vetch, 24 March 1956

Mel Nurse is a name synonymous with Swansea for many reasons. Starting his journey with the club as a member of the ground staff in 1954, he went on to make 257 league appearances for the Swans over two spells between 1955 and 1971. The robust centre-half played alongside some of the most iconic names in Welsh football – Ivor Allchurch, Mel Charles, Cliff Jones and Harry Griffiths, and himself earned 12 caps for Wales. His involvement with the Swans continued after he had retired as a player, where he became a director of the club, saving them from extinction on three separate occasions. There are few men who have done more for Swansea City as a football club, and Mel Nurse rightly wears his nickname 'Mr Swansea' with pride.

Swansea Town: King, Willis, Thomas, Charles, Nurse, Beech, L. Allchurch, Griffiths, Medwin, I. Allchurch, Jones

Leicester City: Anderson, Cunningham, Ogilvie, Froggatt, Fincham, Ward, Riley, Morris, Gardiner, Rowley, Hogg

Swansea Scorers: Terry Medwin (3), Harry Griffiths (2), Len Allchurch

Leicester Scorer: Jack Froggatt

Referee: J. Kelly

Attendance: 16,920

THEY said I was a better cricketer than footballer!

But I only played cricket to keep fit for football. Through the summer months, as a professional footballer, you used to break up at the end of the season and there was at least eight to ten weeks vacant. So, I played cricket all through the summer. I just wanted to keep running.

Today they play football throughout the year, but in our days for eight weeks in the summer there was nothing…bloody hell.

So I joined Highbury, a local team playing with local boys up in Cwmbwrla Park. We used to win the championship practically every year.

We used to have great players in those days. I remember Ray Davies, and Charlie Caswell – he used to play for Glamorgan, but was getting on a bit by then, so he played with us for a bit of fun.

He had these big size 13 boots, and when he ran those 20 yards up to the wicket – BOOM, BOOM, BOOM! – the sound was frightening.

Charlie was 6ft 4in and used to bounce them, but he wasn't as accurate. I was a fast bowler, on the other side from him. I wasn't as fast as him, but I was more accurate and used to grab all the wickets. That's how we played – he used to frighten them to death and I used to take the wickets!

But I didn't want to play cricket. I wanted to play football.

As a kid, I'd spend my life in Cwmbwrla Park. Central to everything in Cwmbwrla, it was fantastic. I would be there all night playing football. When one lot packed it in, I would go over and play with somebody else, then when they packed it in I would go and play with somebody else again. Until the park keeper blew his whistle, shouted 'everybody out', then locked the gate.

After that we would go to Cwmbwrla square and have a cup of tea if we could afford it.

It used to cost me three pence to catch the bus from Cwmbwrla to the bottom of Conway Road up in Penlan. To save that three pence I would run home – that was three or four miles, all uphill! But I thrived on it, I enjoyed it. I kept my three pence in my pocket, nobody was having that off me!

But that was building up my legs and building strength – another means of training. I wasn't necessarily doing it to train, but that's what it was. Everything I've done was with regards to progressing within the sport that I loved.

I always wanted to play football. As a child in infant school I used to play with a tennis ball. I went to Cwmbwrla school and played football for them, then went to Manselton school and played for them too.

While I was in Manselton they sent me up to Ynystawe Park because that's where the schoolboys held their trials and training.

I went up with Mr Morris, who was a teacher in my school linked to the schoolboys. He was a brilliant gentleman who helped me greatly during my time with the schoolboys.

Another player in the school with me was Colin Rees, who also played for Manselton. And there were another two boys, David Davies and Mel Charles, who were in my school, but in different age groups – a bit older than me.

When I went up to Ynystawe, there were boys of 15 years of age, where I was only 14. But I was a tall lad for my age. I was around 5ft 10in when I was in school, there was nobody taller than me. So even though I was only 14, I could hold my own. I was equal to them in size so I could get away with it.

The teacher at the time who used to select the schoolboys was Dai Beynon, from Townhill School. Now, there were loads of boys up there, all different age groups, all from different schools, all congregating at Ynystawe, wanting to play for the schoolboys.

There would be loads of matches, with everyone playing against each other – remove a player, put another one in, remove one, put one in. They were always changing people around to find out the best team.

Practice this was, so Mr Beynon could determine who would be playing for the schoolboys, because they can only have 11 on the field at one time.

At the end of the training, Mr Beynon would stand on a box so he could be above everybody, and he could look out at all the boys who were waiting for him to decide what he was going to do. Who would be representing the schoolboys on the Saturday?

He would call out all these other names, but not mine. I was there, head in my hands, agonising as he kept reeling off these names.

Then he *finally* called my name out. He had selected me!

Mr Beynon actually paid me a compliment many years later. I had finished playing and was sitting outside the front of my hotel, and he walked past. I hadn't seen him for about 50 years, but I instantly recognised him and called out to say hello. We stood talking and at one point he said to me, 'You know what, Mel – when I stood on that box calling out the names, I deliberately left your name until last.'

I'm there looking at him stupid. 'Why did you do that?' I said.

'Because I didn't want you to get carried away with yourself, thinking that you were one of my first selections. Of course, you were, but I left you 'til last.'

Life is funny. If you give a child everything, they get carried away with themselves. Their attitude to life changes.

I was brought up in an ordinary terraced house in Cwmbwrla, changed my shoes once a year, if I was lucky! If there were holes in them, my father would cobble them – with cardboard! – but that was the upbringing I had. And Dai Beynon kept me at that level.

I remember we then moved from Cwmbwrla to Prescelli Road in Penlan. While we were up there I was playing for the Swansea Schoolboys and the Welsh Schoolboys.

I played with some great players in the schoolboys. Every club in the country wanted the Swansea players. Our schoolboys were winning everything.

If you look at the cup – the English trophy that's linked to the schoolboys – on the base of it reads: 'Swansea Town', 'Swansea Town', 'Swansea Town', 'Somebody Else', 'Swansea Town'.

When I saw that, even in those days, I couldn't believe it. Swansea appeared on it more than any other club. Most probably they have new cups today because they couldn't fit any more 'Swansea Towns' on it!

When I left school, I had the option to join four clubs – Arsenal, Chelsea, West Brom and Bristol Rovers. Back then, West Brom and Bristol Rovers were just as dominant as the other two.

Those four came in for me, but nobody from the Swans approached my mother, or my family, or the school, or anybody.

And I didn't want to leave Swansea. I'm a Swansea boy – what did I want to leave Swansea for? I'm playing football, I want to play for Swansea, and that was it. But then I remember this particular game I played for the Welsh Schoolboys. We had played away from home in Ireland. When I came back to Swansea I remember walking up Conway Road with my bag, down Prescelli Road to my house, then I knock the door about nine o'clock at night. After playing away for a week I was glad to get home.

My mum answered the door that night.

'Hello son,' she said. 'There's somebody here from the Swans.'

A big pause.

I couldn't believe it. They sent someone up. They wanted me!

The gentleman sitting in the living room was Glyn Evans. He was a scout for the Swans and a very pleasant fella. He came from the Valleys – we called him Glyn Buff because he was quite stocky, but a real gentleman.

Because he came down from the Rhondda to see me, and I was away in Ireland, he had stayed with my parents for two days. The manager of Swansea Town at the time, Billy McCandless, had seen Glyn and sent him up to our house to ask me if I would like to go down the Vetch.

Would I like to go down the Vetch? That's all I'd dreamt of!

A couple of months later Glyn died in a bus accident on the way back to the Valleys. It was very sad, but I was very grateful to him for coming up and telling me I could start my career at the Vetch.

I joined the Vetch as part of the ground staff at 15 years of age. There were eight of us on the ground staff, all from the schoolboys from different parts of Swansea.

Two out of the eight – those players who the club thought would make the grade – would be in the dressing rooms, helping the players, wiping their backs, getting them towels, getting their boots.

One would be in the first team changing rooms, one in the reserves. The other six players were outside with the groundsmen helping on the field, wheeling soil around, and the rest of it. It was a learning process. It stems from there and you work your way up.

I was out on the grounds at first for around 12 months, but I moved into the dressing room just before they signed me professionally. It was like a promotion!

In those days the club had four teams. First there was the Colts, which was the team for the schoolboys leaving school. It's changed today, because some now play in the first team when they are 17, but in those days that never happened. Very rare that happened – you had to be George Best or John Charles to play at that age.

After the Colts you would progress up to the Welsh League team, then the Combination team, which was the second or reserve team, and then the first team, where the stars would play.

So, I was part of the ground staff and playing for the Colts, and we were great. We used to win all the championships. Then I moved up to play for the Welsh League team facing local teams like Carmarthen, Pembroke, Haverfordwest, and Ton Pentre. It was a fantastic division, playing football around the local communities.

Then I got into the Combination team, which used to play in the Combination competition with teams from across Wales and England. And that's when you really started travelling.

Woah! I wasn't really familiar with travelling. I came from Cwmbwrla – we couldn't afford to go to the beach, let alone travel away!

Every journey away was something different, wherever you went there was something new to see. It was a novelty. Just think of the personal satisfaction of travelling around the country at that age.

In the Combination team I was around 17 years old. I was playing alongside two colleagues – at right-half was Brian Hughes, there was Malcolm Kennedy on the left, and myself at centre-half. We formed a half-back line and we didn't need anyone else on the field. Brian had the flair to go forward, which was a gift – you've either got it or you haven't. Malcolm was the safety player, with me in the middle. I was working off those two – they were brilliant, we had such a balance.

In 1956, the year I was selected for the first team, the first team were practically at the bottom of the Second Division table, while the Combination team was at the top of their table.

Brian, Malcolm and myself were all doing well in the Combination. That was probably why the manager suddenly took the whole half-back line from one team and swapped it over with the other!

It wouldn't happen today. I don't know why, but that's what he did.

It's no surprise that the Combination team suddenly started losing their form and the first team began going up the table!

And that's around the time we played Leicester City at home, which was my first game for Swansea.

At that stage, me and my family were living in a council house in Gendros. I was very fortunate that a few doors away from us lived a gentleman called Les Bailey, who worked as a writer for the *Evening Post*.

I can remember the night before the Leicester game we were in the house watching the telly. I was going to bed at nine, as I had to get up early in the morning to get down the Vetch. I was a fanatic, nothing was going to get in my way – football, football, football, that was all I was focused on.

All of a sudden, the front doorbell rings. Ding, ding. It was Les Bailey. We invited him in, where he delivered some news. He explained that the centre-half at the time, Tom Kiley, had had an injury with his ankle and he had hobbled off in training, so he was not going to be playing in the Leicester game.

So, they improvised. Ronnie Burgess was the player-manager at that time, after Billy McCandless had died in March the previous year, and he had chosen to put me in the first team. Les was one of the first to know it as he was so heavily linked to the club.

And who were we playing against? Leicester City.

They were a team that had all the big names at that time – Arthur Rowley, who was called 'The Gunner'. He scored around 250 goals in 300 games. They also had Willie Gardiner, another top goalscorer playing for them. These men were legends. And Leicester were top of the table, trying to get back in to the First Division.

And they were going to put me in as a 17-year-old?

But I was never afraid to go on the field. I was self-confident, not arrogant. I was so sure of myself. You have to be, and it has to come naturally. Some players will step on the field with all the ability in the world but they can't perform. When they get in front of a big crowd, they are knackered.

And we had big crowds. In those days football was *the* thing – it was like the Swans now in the Premier League.

In those days there was not much seating – only the Centre Stand and the West Stand had seating. There was no shelter on the East Stand or the North Bank. Just open banks. But we averaged around 25,000 to 30,000 people a game, standing.

But it was cheap – tickets were reasonable then. That was the only income the club had coming in, through gate money.

That's why there was a maximum wage – £20 and that's your lot. And it was only the privileged first team that would get that amount.

Football wasn't a money game in those days. You have to live, but players weren't going to finish their football careers with millions of pounds in the bank. If they could finish their careers owning their own house, even with a mortgage, they would be grateful. But in our days, you weren't playing for money, you were playing for the love of the game.

We didn't actually have that big a crowd for the Leicester game, just a small gate of around 17,000. The crowd were depleted because the team were depleted. Because Tom Kiley was injured and one or two others weren't playing, it was just expected that Leicester were going to thrash the Swans. Some people didn't want to turn up for that.

Leicester were at the top and we were down at the bottom, struggling. It was a foregone conclusion that they were going to hammer us. But the reverse happened that day.

They had actually beaten us badly earlier in the season – 6-1 was the score, although I wasn't playing that day. But on 24 March, we went and beat *them* 6-1!

Now, you've got to turn the clock back and think about how you felt at the age of 17. You can imagine how nervous I was. I was a young kid, thrown in the deep end with all these legends. And, being a local boy, playing for a local team is something you dream about.

What a team we had. Len Allchurch – 'The Fox', we called him, because he was so clever and cunning. A great player. Terry Medwin – a great player. Ivor Allchurch – a legend, a great player. Harry Griffiths – a great player. Jonny King was in goal at the time. He was a nice lad from up the Valleys and a great player.

They were mostly local boys in that team, although Ronnie Burgess and Arthur Willis had come from Spurs. Willis was a full-back and Ronnie was a left-half.

On that day I was playing in defence alongside Arthur Willis, Gilbert Beech, who was left-back, and Dai Thomas, who was right-back. They were quality players too.

I was a bit cautious talking to all those players because they were at the top and I was down at the bottom, just coming through. Who was I to talk to those great players?

You were aware of your position, but you went out and did your best.

That's what I did in the game against Leicester. I could only give my best, but I had to because I wanted to progress.

Playing among quality players like those around me, you have every chance of doing something good. I wasn't a timid player, I was an aggressive player and that's what the Swans needed. That Leicester game suited me down to the ground because I had quality around me and I was aggressive in my attitude.

Don't forget, in those days you were playing in the mud, it wasn't turf. Centre-halves were six foot-odd, and centre-forwards were six foot-odd.

Every time a challenge for the ball came in – WHAM! – there were bodies flying.

I used to go in quite hard but I wasn't the only one, everybody did. They would come in at me and I would go in at them. That's why, throughout my career, I split my eyes, broke my nose, and spent plenty of time in hospital.

On my debut game we only let in one goal, which was scored by their left-half Jack Froggatt. But we scored six that day! Terry Medwin scored a hat-trick, Harry Griffiths had two, and Len Allchurch took the other. It was a brilliant result.

Five games later I had to go to the army to do my National Service, which lasted two years. But it was a way of life, everybody had to do it. You knew when you turned 18 years of age, you had to do National Service.

I didn't want to do it, I wanted to play with the Swans. But you had to go.

Over the two years you spend doing National Service you grow up – you go from a boy to a man. I needed those two years to grow up. How I would have turned out otherwise, if I hadn't done that, I don't know.

I came out of the army in 1958 and went back to the Vetch, to re-join my old team-mates. I have lots of funny stories about my time with the Swans, but I remember this one well.

As I mentioned earlier, we had moved down from Prescelli Road to Gendros. Mel Charles used to live in a house in Gwylym Street, near me. Right opposite his house was a bus stop.

On this particular day we were playing at home, and we would both catch the bus to the Vetch from Gendros. Nobody had cars in our days – you were lucky if you had a bike!

I'd usually catch the bus from the top end of the road. That's if you could get on the bus… they would be packed with people because everybody would be going to the Vetch!

This day in particular I was waiting at the bus stop.

To be honest, I wouldn't usually stand in the bus queue, or you'd have too many people saying hello and asking for autographs. I would wait for the bus around the corner, and when it came I would run like hell and jump on the platform!

We would go down the road about 200 yards, turn right and there would be Mel Charles waiting at his bus stop.

So, this day, I shouted, 'Keep going driver!'

Because if I got there before Charlo I'd most probably have been the 12th man – the one sub. I wasn't a regular in the first team then, but I'd have been 12th man. If anybody cried off injured, I'd be playing. So, if I could leave Charlo behind, I'd be playing that day.

Anyway, the bus carried on, passing Mel because it was full.

The bus dropped me off in town. I walked up through the centre and came around the corner to the Vetch, where I could see huge queues of people waiting to get into the ground.

Poor Charlo was still stuck up in Gendros!

Now, there used to be a lot of rag and bone men years ago, selling firewood and all that. One of them men was coming along and Charlo had shouted to him, 'Give us a lift into town – I'm playing this afternoon and the buses are full!'

So, he jumped on the horse and cart, and came down to town. You can imagine all the people queuing to go into the Vetch, doing a double-take as they saw one of their star players hurtle past sitting on the horse and cart! 'Rag and bone!'

But that was the way of life in our time.

In 1962 I bought a house on the promenade, but within two months of me buying the house, the club sold me to Middlesbrough.

A lot of people say I asked for a transfer. But I never asked for a transfer from Swansea. Never. Why should I want to move from Swansea? Why would I buy a house if I wanted to move? That's the truth.

I didn't want to go. Not to be nasty to Middlesbrough, but I didn't want to go there. Manchester United and Manchester City wanted to buy me too. Loads of clubs wanted to buy me. But I didn't want to go anywhere. In those days I wanted to play for Swansea, and I didn't want to leave my mother and father.

But I was working. Football was work. And Middlesbrough put me on a pedestal, made me club skipper, player of the year… For the three or four years I was there I was lucky. I was captain of the club and if players didn't listen to me they'd have trouble!

After Middlesbrough, I ended up playing with Swindon for a few years, but then I came back to Swansea in 1968.

I finished playing professional football in Swansea, but then I went to Pembroke, played for them for a while, then up to Merthyr with big John Charles, and then I finished. I played in some charity games, but that was all. I knew what I was doing. I could have carried on. I was only 32 when I finished, but it wasn't viable for me to continue.

I believe that practically everything that happened to me was meant to happen. I'm very lucky, I'm a very privileged person. I can honestly say this – my life was planned for me. Every time something happens to me I say, 'Cor, I was lucky.'

I've been rewarded for playing football by the city I love. I also feel lucky because the public still remember me.

There's only one place for me, and that's Swansea. I won't even go to Port Talbot because it's outside the radius of the city!

In fact, as a family, we've never been on holiday.

Only once we attempted a holiday. We went to the Isle of Wight for what was supposed to be a fortnight, but we were only there for a few hours, then jumped back on the same ferry. I didn't want to go. I didn't feel comfortable.

In 2016, I was awarded the freedom of the city, and at the time I made this statement. I only went out of Swansea when playing football and doing my National Service. Those two factors compelled me to leave the city.

Other than that, I'm not going anywhere. I ain't leaving Swansea.

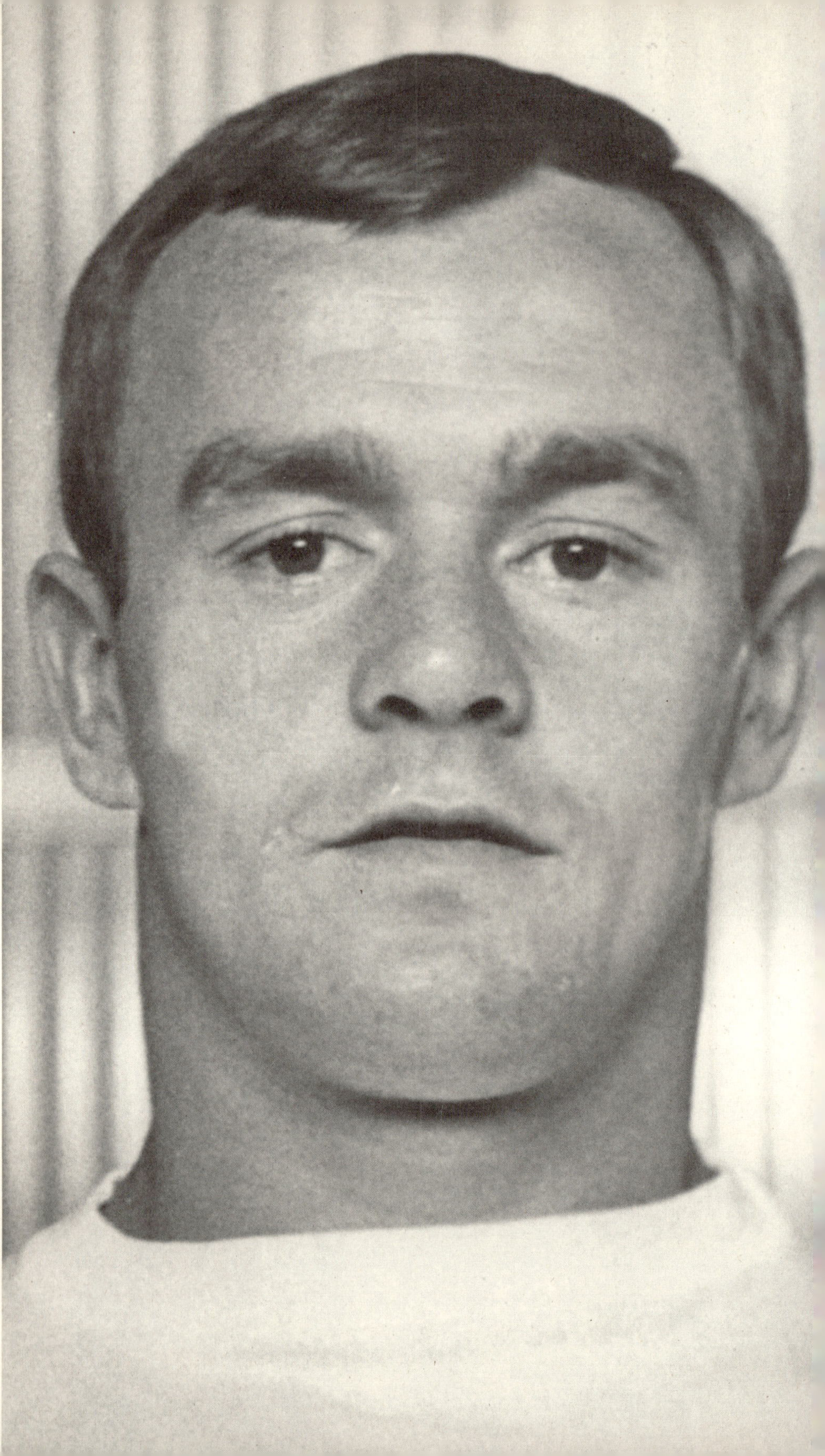

VIC GOMERSALL: BORN 17 JUNE 1942, MANCHESTER; 178 GAMES, 6 GOALS

Vic Gomersall

Swansea Town 0-1 Arsenal
FA Cup Fourth Round
The Vetch, 17 February 1968

Affectionately known as The General, Vic Gomersall was a popular and influential defender for Swansea Town, playing more than 200 games in all competitions. He joined the club from Manchester City for £5,000 in August 1966 and was a regular part of the team thanks to his tenacious tackling and hard work-rate. Although times were tough for Swansea, Vic played his role in some memorable matches and was crowned Player of the Year for the 1967/68 season. He left the club for non-league Chelmsford City in 1971, although he returned to Swansea as commercial manager in 1975, spending 12 years in the position. Vic is still associated with the Swans more than 50 years later, as a matchday host at the Liberty Stadium.

Swansea Town: John, Evans, Gomersall, Williams, Purcell, Davis, Humphries, Allchurch, Todd, Screen, Evans

Arsenal: Furnell, Storey, Simpson, McLintock, Neill, Ure, Radford, Gould, Graham, Sammels, Armstrong

Arsenal Scorer: Gould

Referee: P.R. Walters

Attendance: 32,786

THAT afternoon, the Vetch was absolutely packed with fans. You couldn't have squeezed any more in. They were in the banks, they were up the pylons and they were on the roof.

Honestly, how they got on the roof, I don't know.

It was the record attendance for a Swansea home game. A record that still stands today – you're not going to get 32,000 people in the Liberty Stadium!

When I go to the Liberty now and see a sell-out crowd, I still find it hard to believe that there were half as many again crammed into the Vetch that day. But everyone in the town wanted to be at the game because it was so special for us. We were such a small club back then, stuck in the Fourth Division, so to draw someone like the mighty Gunners, who were indeed one of the top teams in the country at the time – one of the top teams in Europe – was huge. It was just a special day all round.

Once the draw for the fourth round had been announced, the town was absolutely buzzing. Everywhere you went, it was, 'What do you think about the game Vic?'

Nowadays you don't see the players, never mind speak to them, but in those days, we would go to the Vice President's Lounge at the Vetch and chat to the supporters, or you'd see them in town. Being a player, people would recognise you.

After training, quite a few of us would go to the Union Café for beans on toast and a cup of coffee, and fans would come in and say, 'What do you reckon then, who's going to win?'

All I could say was, 'We'll give it a good go!'

Because this was Arsenal. We weren't going to outplay them by any stretch of the imagination – although at times in the game, we actually did.

It was the anticipation ahead of the game that made it so magical. The town was alive. The club shop had sold more scarves and badges prior to that game than ever before. I could tell from the atmosphere in the ground and around the town that this was a big, big game for Swansea.

We weren't doing very well as a football club at the time. We just weren't very good. We had been relegated in 1965 and came down to the Third Division, then we had been relegated again from the Third to the Fourth in '67. As a team, our cohesion wasn't that clever.

And that year we weren't exactly setting the league on fire either, so this cup match was the big highlight of the season.

Arsenal, on the other hand, were near the top of the First Division table at the time, so there was quite a big difference in quality.

Their team was full of big names and I think eight of them were internationals. You had solid, committed defenders like Frank McLintock and Peter Storey, with George Armstrong in the middle, and dangerous forwards like big George Graham and Bobby Gould.

I had come up against Arsenal before when playing for Manchester City in '61, but not against this kind of quality.

That afternoon I would be marking John Radford, who was one of Arsenal's greatest ever players. For a winger, he was a big, strong boy. In those days, wingers weren't very big – they were usually slight and quick.

He was a good player with both his head and his feet. I think he played for England if my memory serves me right, so I had to be on my best game that day.

I know he beat me once or twice, but I probably intercepted balls to him and tackled him once or twice too. At the end of the day, I suppose it was 50-50 between us.

Compared to that lot we were an average side, but we had some good talent, like Brian Evans, who was a Welsh international winger, and Herbie Williams who had been with Swansea for years. And, of course, Ivor Allchurch was the stand-out player for us.

Ivor was a lovely, lovely man and a great player. He was called the Golden Boy of Welsh Soccer, which was a thoroughly deserved title. He was the complete package – a strong player with big thighs, skilful on the ball, could shoot with either foot, and score with his head. A great, great player. What he would be worth nowadays, with these extortionate fees, I dread to think.

Ivor was revered in football. In fact, I remember inside the *Charles Buchan's Football Monthly* – a magazine I used to have as a tot – they had a photograph of Ivor in his black and white Newcastle shirt, which I stuck on my bedroom wall. And yet I finished up playing with him, which was absolutely brilliant.

It was his second time with the club. I wasn't there the first time he played, back in the 1950s. Maybe he had lost a little bit of his sharpness, but he was still a wonderful player.

I couldn't give him enough accolades to be honest. It was a pleasure and an absolute honour for me to play alongside Ivor Allchurch – and his brother Len, who was just as lovely. Without doubt, they were two of the nicest people I ever met in football.

Other than that, we had lads who enjoyed the game and had ability, but just weren't good enough to get to the top.

While we weren't the best players, the camaraderie in the dressing room was great and everybody was good mates.

When it came to training and preparation before the match, we didn't do a great deal different to usual. There was no point putting extra stuff in, as you want to save your energy for the game itself.

That's what I can't understand about footballers today. They go out on to the pitch before the match and start running around – they're using up ten per cent of their energy right there!

In our days, you'd be in the dressing room with your foot on the table to do your stretches, and that was that.

There's so many injuries now, you never used to have them back then. There's so many muscles they've got now I never even knew we had!

We had played a match the Saturday before, so would have had a day off on the Monday. Then on the Tuesday we would have a good day training, to get all the aches and pains out. We would have also done a lighter session on the Wednesday – maybe seven-a-side with the squad that would be involved on the day. Then Thursday you'd have an easier day. We would just do a couple of laps to warm up, because invariably you'd have had to run up to the Mumbles and back along the beach.

We'd also train on the Friday afternoon. We'd do a couple of 'doggies', which were running to different cones placed at ten yards, 20 yards, 30 yards, and back. Then maybe you'd go and have a game of tennis, just for a bit of fun.

I remember there were one or two incidents leading up to the game.

It was the university's rag week, with the students out celebrating. On the Friday night before the game, some of them had broken into the Vetch and sawn through the goalposts!

First thing on the Saturday morning, Syd Tucker – our groundsman – goes on the pitch to get it ready, and noticed the posts were wonky. They were still standing but had been cut clean through. So, Syd and the groundsmen did some quick repairs to reinforce the posts in time for the big match.

There was another incident that was quite sad really. One of our programme sellers was in Picton Arcade selling his programmes and he got beaten up rather badly, with all his programmes and money taken. We had heard about it before the game, and we weren't too happy about that.

But after all that drama we were ready for the game.

We came out on to the pitch and were greeted by a mass of faces. What a tremendous atmosphere, and the noise was absolutely deafening. The Vetch was a wonderful ground for atmosphere anyway, but that day was different.

Fortunately, I had played in similar circumstances for Man City, but for some of the lads who had never played in that atmosphere, it was quite an experience.

They were only getting a couple of thousand fans through the gates those days, so having 32,000 supporters cheering them on was something else.

Going into the game we knew we had to be realistic, work hard, close them down, put them under pressure, and go from there.

But as you may expect, it was us who were under pressure from the start of the game, as Arsenal showed their authority.

They had some good chances quite early on, and I played my part in keeping the scores level. I remember heading clear a ball that was goal-bound, and then around the 20th minute, when Radford was through all of our players, I managed to just get in front of him and knock the ball away for a corner.

George Graham had some chances too, but I also helped put a stop to those. One of the reporters for the paper wrote something like, 'Graham was through on goal, and it was only the speed of Gomersall that saved the day.'

We were a bit under the cosh, but then we gradually came into the game.

In the first half we had some chances of our own through Ivor Allchurch, Billy Screen and Willy Humphries, who almost caught Arsenal's goalkeeper Jim Furnell off guard. One of Screen's long shots sailed inches over the crossbar, and you could see Arsenal were relieved.

We had given them a good game in the first half and it was 50-50, although we could see Arsenal had that little bit more finesse. There was that little touch of class, whereas our game was more about getting among them, and if you could manage to kick them, all the better!

But it was end-to-end, we had a little bit of play in the middle of the first half, then they came back at the start of the second half.

The saddest thing, which still upsets me to this day, came at the start of the second half. We were on the attack and were really pressurising them – so much so that we scored.

The ball came across, Herbie Williams headed it down, and Toddy knocked it in the net. Well, the crowd erupted didn't it, but the referee disallowed it. He reckoned Herbie had pushed one of their defenders as he jumped.

But if you look at the photos, you can see Herbie is leaning backwards with his arms down by his sides as the ball is coming across. Perhaps the ref saw something we didn't, but it was so disappointing.

Two minutes later, they get the ball and Graham sent in a cross. Joe Davis was in the centre but was a bit out of position and didn't get hold of it. I had tried to sprint back, but Bobby Gould was there to nod it into the back of the net.

And that was devastating, especially after we had just had our goal disallowed.

Maybe it caught us on the hop because we went from ecstatic to deflated within seconds. We may have lost a little bit of concentration, and of course they would have taken advantage of anything like that.

We had around half an hour left to get something from the game, and we put them under severe pressure, pinning them back in their own half for much of it. Their keeper made a couple of good saves. Ivor was unlucky – I remember he hit a shot toward the goal and I thought, 'This is going in,' but Furnell dived across and got his fingertips to it. I remember thinking, 'Oh, get out of the way!' followed by some expletives.

We lost the match through that single goal, but, at the end of the day, we came off with our heads held high. We were the underdog who had given it everything.

Arsenal's manager, Bertie Mee, came into the dressing room after the match and said, 'Lads, you played really well, and put us under a lot of pressure. We were fortunate to come away with the win. You could have been taking us back to our ground for the replay.'

We wouldn't have minded a trip to Highbury. We may have been beaten by six or seven there at Arsenal, but it would have been nice to go.

I think Ivor had been there, but players like Herbie – who'd been with the Swans for his entire career – he had never experienced First Division football.

Highbury was a fabulous ground. They had underfloor heating in the dressing rooms. At the Vetch, we just had that bloody big boiler in the middle of our dressing room.

We were disappointed after the effort we'd put in, but it was just one of those games.

If the ref had allowed our goal to stand, that would have lifted us. We would have gone for another. Then they may have panicked a little bit, and we may have taken advantage again. Who knows what would have happened.

We were unlucky, but all right – you've got to accept it.

Actually, we had a similar thing at Leeds in the FA Cup third round in 1970, which was harder to accept. This is when they were talking about Don Revie influencing referees.

We took the lead in the first half. Big Dai Gwyther got the goal, and we were way on top. We gave them what for and really played well.

But then, late in the second half, Mel Nurse went down to head a ball, Allan Clarke came up with his studs and kicked him in the chest. You could see spots of blood coming through Nursey's shirt.

So Nursey gave him a big elbow on his shoulder – WHACK. Clarke went down holding his face, and got Nurse sent off. Mick Jones scored with a header from a cross with two minutes to go.

This was undeserved and came ten minutes after Leeds had been awarded a penalty for a handball by David Lawrence, which wasn't handball at all. In fact, Terry Cooper came in from behind and pushed Dai in the back. Dai went over, along with Cooper, and the penalty was awarded.

We all sarcastically clapped the referee off at the end of the match. We could have been reprimanded for that, but we were so dejected and annoyed, we didn't care. It was unbelievable.

I remember their chairman Leslie Silver came into the dressing room and said, 'Gentlemen, you were robbed. I am most embarrassed by my team. You fully deserved to win.'

Nice of him to say it, but it was no good to us, as we'd lost 2-1. Two referees cocked it up for us in the cup within two years.

But that's the game.

I always did my best to be an honest player, all my career. Nobody could say, 'You've never tried.' Of course, I had bad games – I would be telling lies if I said I didn't. But I was a one hundred per cent player. I was quick and I had a good left foot, and I used to work hard.

I was having bad times when I first came to the Swans. I had come from Man City where I had more time on the ball to have a look up and see where I was going to pass.

I played like a crab for the first half-dozen games at Swansea! But the crowd never got on to me, fair play, and I soon settled.

The fans at the Vetch were brilliant, they loved me. I used to sprint down the flank to attack and stick my chest out as I ran. I had a barrel chest, which was something I developed as a kid. The fans used to call me 'Chesty'.

Originally, I wasn't going to join Swansea, but I'm glad I did. I came down under Glyn Davies after realising I wouldn't play much more with Manchester City.

I had signed a new contract at City, but I spoke to Joe Mercer, who was manager at the time, and he told me he couldn't promise I would play.

I'd had a taste of first team football and I just wanted to play, so I thought I could work at getting in the team at Man City or go play regularly at Swansea. So, I came to Swansea.

In my five seasons at Swansea, I played under a few different managers, but it was Billy Lucas in charge for the big Arsenal match. He was a great character, and football was his life. He never used to call the ball a ball – he would call it a 'tater. 'Get that 'tater straight up the line,' he used to say.

He was a short, stocky boy. A Welsh international and a good player. But a dirty player – he used to put himself about. In them days, you had to.

But it was honest back then, nothing like it is nowadays, where the players fall over at nothing.

It was solid football. You'd hear the crowd go 'oooh' at every 50-50 ball. You don't hear that now.

To relate to this story, I do a fair bit of after-dinner compering up in Penlan. I've had all the hard men join me – Emlyn Hughes, Nobby Stiles, Chopper Harris, Norman Hunter and Tommy Smith.

I did an event with Tommy Smith a few years ago, who I had known from his time at Swansea.

We were talking, and he said, 'These days, you see a player get clipped and they go down crying and rolling over. If I was still playing, I know for a fact that I would have gone over while they were laying on the floor, given them such a boot in the thigh, and said, "Now fucking roll over." Then I would have walked off the pitch, because I would have obviously been given a red card after that.'

It's brilliant, and I hear so many stories on the circuit. Honestly, if I had a retentive memory, I would be the best comedian in the world!

I had a great time playing more than 200 games for Swansea but left in 1971 when I was going on 30.

I was nearly going to go to Southport where Jimmy Meadows was manager, as it was closer to Manchester, but there was a bit of a battle for my signature from Chelmsford and Kettering.

There was lots of to-ing and fro-ing, and the signing-on fee kept increasing from both. Eventually I went to Chelmsford with Dave Bumpstead, signing on for £3,000 in the end.

Chelmsford were actually a non-league side, but we won the Southern League championship the year I joined. Sadly, the club were banned from applying for league status for five years, because they had broken some FA transfer rules two years previously. Otherwise we would have been promoted and I would have been back in the Football League. Instead, that year, Hereford entered the Football League despite finishing runners-up to us.

I still follow Chelmsford now, but they're not as good as they used to be.

After four years with them I finished playing due to my knee injury but was still with Chelmsford on the commercial side of things.

I returned to Swansea in 1975, when the Swans were having a big anniversary at the Vetch – a big cavalcade of sport they called it – and they invited 20 former players from previous years like Ivor, Lenny, Nursey, Cliff Jones, Terry Medwin and myself, to play in an exhibition match.

On the day, after the match, Malcom Struel came over to me and said, 'You fancy coming back down here to work with us in the commercial department? We've heard what a great job you've done at Chelmsford.'

How he knew that I'll never know, but I decided that I would be happy to come back down to Wales.

I ended up spending 12 years on the commercial side of things at Swansea, working with Bobby Jones, who was the commercial director at the time.

We had a great time. Bobby was a good man and earned a lot of money for the club – a lot of people didn't know that. He was a big factor in the commercial success of the Swans.

I helped the club a lot when it came to raising money, and worked on lots of projects, like the 500 Club. There were 500 members, each member would pay a pound, then we would have a draw every week for around £250. We actually had a waiting list to join the 500 Club, it was that successful. It was a good income for the club.

I also created and ran the Moonraker lottery – and it was unbelievable. It was a scratchcard, with eight symbols on it. If you got three of the same you would get a prize, whether that was a pound or a thousand. It was going all over Milford, Haverfordwest, Pembroke, Bridgend…It was like shelling peas to be honest because things were going so well for the club. They were good times.

We were selling 45,000 tickets a week, making £12,500 revenue for the club every week! Because it was a sell-out, there was a £1,000 winner every week – and that was a lot of money back then.

But it was with this money that the club could go out and buy your Tommy Smiths and Ian Callaghans. Some people don't realise this.

I remember in 1979 we also ran a competition for a song for Swansea City, from the club shop on William Street. The winner was 'Swansea, oh Swansea' by Roger Evans, a lad from Llanelli. I was the one who initiated that.

We had quite a few entries, but it was a toss-up between two tapes. One from Roger, and another one, but I can't remember the name of the fella who wrote it.

The song from Roger was my favourite, but the only thing going against that one was the section that went, 'In the League Cup, there came Tottenham, who were lucky to draw the game.' Then it went on about Ardiles and company. And I thought, 'Will that reference still be relevant in five or ten years' time?'

The other song never mentioned any particular game, it was just about the club in general.

But we went with the one from Roger, because it was so catchy.

I was worried if it would last five years, but 40 years on they're still singing it! Although I still don't know why the fans don't change the lyrics to 'Take me to the Liberty, way down by the sea' – they still sing about the Vetch.

At the same time as my commercial work, I was also working on the Tannoy system at the Vetch, doing the public addresses for games, announcing the teams, playing records, and that kind of thing. I used to sit in the little press compartment at the top left-hand side of the main stand.

I always used to have a bit of fun with the crowd when I was announcing things. But apparently Malcolm Struel wasn't keen on this, and one day he had said to Bobby Jones, 'Tell Vic to cut down on the comedy bit – it's a serious job.'

So, soon after, I made another announcement to the crowd. It was when we were in the Second Division, when Tosh was in charge.

It was a Saturday. I forget who we were playing, but on the Tuesday night we would be at home again, against Watford who were top of the table. We were second, so it was going to be a significant game in our push for promotion.

At half-time, my voice boomed across the Vetch. 'Ladies and gentlemen, don't forget we've got a big game on Tuesday night,' I said. 'We know there's going to be a big crowd, and the club have spared no expense in making sure you supporters are comfortable – that's why we have ordered another two dozen meat pies!'

The crowd cheered loudly, 'Whey!'

Of course, Malcolm Struel didn't think it was funny.

But this is why I got on so well with the supporters. I think lots of people were appreciative that I had gone back to the club after I had finished playing. Considering I was an Englishman, the Swans fans were great to me!

These days I do the matchday hosting in the LT10 at the Liberty Stadium, which means I am still associated with the club after 51 years.

I'm proud to still work at a wonderful football club that has given me so much happiness over the years. Swansea is definitely home for me now.

DAVID GWYTHER: BORN 6 DECEMBER 1948, BIRMINGHAM; 216 GAMES, 60 GOALS

David Gwyther

Oxford City 1-5 Swansea Town

FA Cup Second Round

The White House Ground, 6 December 1969

When it comes to goals, David Gwyther scored his fair share for Swansea Town, and City – in fact, he was the scorer of the very first Swansea City goal, after the club changed its name in early 1970. Born in Birmingham, Gwyther's family returned to Swansea before his first birthday, where he grew up in Penclawdd. After joining the Swans as an apprentice, the powerful striker cemented his position in the starting XI under Glyn Davies. The prolific target man was a fans' favourite and scored 60 goals in the league over more than 200 appearances, becoming the Swans' top goalscorer for three consecutive seasons (1969/70, 70/71 and 71/72). Although he left Swansea City for Halifax in 1973, Gwyther eventually returned to the city he grew up in after retiring from the game.

Swansea Town: Millington, Slee, Gomersall, Williams, Nurse, Screen, Allchurch, Slattery, Williams, Gwyther, Evans

Oxford City: Hawkins, Ramsden (Wiffen), Keay, Morton, Shufflebotham, Metcalfe, Eatwell, Woodley, Oram, Pentecoste, Booker

Swansea Scorers: Gwyther (4), Evans

Oxford Scorer: Woodley

Referee: D.R. Nippard

Attendance: 3,800

I HADN'T told anyone that it was my 21st birthday.

I was quite shy in them days, especially playing with some magnificent players, who were heroes to me at Swansea.

I just wanted to focus on the match, as the FA Cup was a big thing back then.

We would call it 'cup week' and it was always a special time compared to preparing for a league game, because we'd do things a bit differently.

Some days during cup week, the club would take us on the bus, then drop us off somewhere in Pennard, and we'd have a walk, then a jog to Langland and Caswell. Then we would play a five-a-side match on the beach, then go have some soup or something.

Anything different, and it would be lovely.

The FA Cup was exciting for players and supporters, but just as welcomed by the club because they would get a lot of money if we drew a big team. I think the clubs used to share the money, so a big gate would be great for both clubs.

You would also have the League Cup, which was always a midweek game, and they were still quite important because the clubs could make a few bob on them too.

But the FA Cup saw the Swans get some big teams, so back then it meant something to get through to the next round.

In the competition we faced some major clubs like Liverpool and Leeds – who we went on to play after Oxford City – which was why the win against Oxford was so important.

I had always been a supporter of the Swans growing up. My family were from Penclawdd originally, although I was born in Birmingham as my father was working in a factory up there at the time.

But we moved back down to Wales when I was 11 months old, so Swansea has always been my home. I grew up in Upper Killay and went to Penclawdd school, although didn't play football with the school – they were rugby-only, as it tended to be in them days.

I began playing football at Swansea YMCA, then moved on to play with the senior league team for Fairwood Rangers when I was 13 years old. That was a very young age to be playing in such a hard league. When they disbanded, most of us went down to continue playing with South Gower FC, when I was around 15.

Growing up, I was planning to do an apprenticeship in plastering, but word spread that I was a decent footballer and was scoring regularly, so the father of one of my friends took me down to the Vetch to meet the manager, Glyn Davies. Nothing came of it originally, but then I found out they wanted me down there on the ground staff as an apprentice. From there I signed pro at 17, and then stayed with Swansea until I was 24.

It was a different system back there. I worked on the old ground with Syd, the groundsman at the time. There would be about three of us out there helping him, and three sorting the stands and doing other jobs.

I was lucky because I was doing all right in some of the training matches, so the manager told me he wanted me to train with the reserves and the first team. I made my debut with the first team against Brighton and Hove [Albion] at the very end of the 1965/66 season, and then became a regular at around 19.

We had some great players in the late 1960s. None more magical than Ivor Allchurch.

Ivor was my idol, and a superb player. Even though he was coming to the end of his career as I was starting, he did some things on the field that were just amazing.

He was so comfortable on the ball and very clever. He was also a surprisingly strong player, but he never fouled people. On and off the field he was a lovely character and really down to earth. I hope I've turned out the same as him, as he was a great role model for me.

Herbie Williams was another one I looked up to. Herbie was one of the greats at Swansea as far as I'm concerned.

To be honest, I think Herbie was a very underrated player, as some of the things he did in training and games in them days were brilliant. But he had a bad knee injury earlier in his career and they reckon that had affected his confidence a bit.

We also had players like Len Allchurch, Brian Evans, and Mel Nurse, who had come back to Swansea after playing for Swindon. There was Tony Millington in goal, Barrie Hole, and Geoff Thomas – he was a good player too. Man United wanted him after a loan spell there, but he was a real home bird.

Although I used to play football as a kid on the Saturday, I would still rush down to the Vetch afterwards to catch the second half of the Swans game. We used to walk in at half-time; you wouldn't have to pay anything then.

So, it was brilliant to join Swansea, and to be training and playing with some of the greats like Ivor, Len and Herbie. It was a wonderful feeling.

By the time we went to take on Oxford City in the second round of the FA Cup in 1969, I had been with the club for around four years. I was young compared to the players today, but even at 21 I was a regular in the first team.

These days they have specific under-23 teams, but if you haven't made it into the first team by the time you are 23, you haven't got much chance.

I was a strong, bustling centre-forward and was playing quite well, with a lot of clubs after me at that stage. I had a good spell of scoring goals in the league, the FA Cup, and the Welsh Cup, and I was well known for scoring a hat-trick.

In December 1969, we were getting results in the league, and eventually went on to win promotion from the Fourth to the Third Division at the end of the season.

We had a great team and a good manager in Roy Bentley. Roy was one of the best managers I played under, because he had been a striker himself. He had been a big goalscorer for Chelsea and played for England in the 1950 World Cup.

The boys used to call me his favourite actually. 'Look, his pet is coming,' the others would say. He used to spend a lot of time out with me on the field in training, working on shooting and striking the ball. He was a good manager and a lovely man.

Roy came to us from Reading after he was sacked by them. I remember we hammered them 5-0 in a league game at the Vetch in March 1971 and I scored a hat-trick – that's probably why I became his pet!

Despite the season-long target of promotion in the league, on 6 December 1969 – the day of my 21st birthday – all eyes were fixed on getting past Oxford in the cup.

Earlier in the season we had played Kettering Town in the first round. Herbie scored both goals in a 2-0 win, and that's how we got to the second round against Oxford City. Oxford were an Isthmian League team, and they had done well to get to where they were in the cup that season. It was one of those matches that could have been a banana skin for us.

It was quite a small crowd at their ground that winter's day, but there was still a great atmosphere because we had a lot of Swans fans up there.

It was a horrible Saturday afternoon, with lots of rain, although the wind wasn't too bad. I used to love those kind of games, because the defenders and keepers would be slipping around and making mistakes, with me there to follow them in – it was a forward's dream really.

The pitches back then were terrible sometimes, especially at the non-league grounds. Look at the Liberty Stadium pitch today and that's just wonderful as it runs so true.

Back then, the ball would come across, you would go to kick it, it would hit a bobble, jump away from your foot and you would miss it completely. The crowd would be groaning and shouting at you, but there was nothing you could do!

The Vetch was a lot better than those pitches in non-league. We used to think the Vetch was brilliant at the start of every season, but it used to cut up quite badly too – the two wings would go, then the centre circle and around the goalmouths.

But this was the case with most pitches back then unless you were in the First Division. Even then, the bigger clubs had to sand their pitches to help absorb water and cover any ruts.

Before we went out to start the match, I remember the manager telling us to go out and knock them low and hard across the box. Those were his instructions – low and hard.

Because of the poor conditions and the churned-up pitch, the keeper would be more likely to drop the ball after catching it, and we would be there to knock them in. They weren't bad tactics from him, but we had no success with that against Oxford.

I think we tried to follow his instructions in the first half, but it didn't work because, not only did we fail to score, but we conceded! Oxford ended up scoring around half an hour into the match, through their forward John Woodley. We didn't equalise, so went in at half-time trailing 1-0.

That was a big surprise for me – for all of us, as no one expected them to be on top that day. I can imagine what our supporters were thinking at half-time.

I've played against a lot of non-league teams and the plan was to always get an early goal to take the sting out their tails. That's why letting Oxford score was a bit dodgy to say the least.

But we came out for the second half and I scored four goals – all from my head – to completely turn the game around.

The tactics of hitting them low and hard just wasn't working. It was a mucky old pitch and it was getting very cut up, so Len Allchurch started sending them in high. And that worked.

That wasn't the only game I scored a lot of goals thanks to Len's accurate crossing of the ball. We had a good understanding of each other.

I knew that once he got into the last third of the pitch he would be sending in a cross, and I had to get on to the far post to either head towards goal or back across the goal, for the midfielders running into the box.

Len used to say to me, 'If I knock a cross in and you're not there, you'll have a bollocking!'

He used to wind me up because I was younger, but I knew I had to be there to make contact with it.

We had him on one wing, and Brian Evans on the other, and they were different kinds of players.

When Len got into the last third, the ball was always coming over the top. But with Brian he would beat the full-back, jink it and cut back, so I had to delay my run. I worked well with both of them and would time my runs so I could get to the back post.

Today I see so many balls going across the box then past the far post with nobody on the end of them. That does my head in.

That day against Oxford I remember the goals well. I seemed to score every ten minutes. The first one came in the 52nd minute, then the 62nd, then the 74th, then a final one in the final minute of the match.

Brian Evans also scored a goal for us in the 72nd minute. I actually almost nabbed that one as well, but he just nipped in before me. I guess I couldn't be too greedy!

Eventually, it ended 5-1 to us, which was more like the result we expected before the match.

The Swansea supporters who had travelled up were thrilled. I know it was a game against lower opposition, but you still had to win the game at the end of the day. So, after the final whistle went, before I could get into the dressing room, the crowd lifted me above their heads and carried me off the pitch, singing the song, 'Gwyther is our king!'

It was all a bit of a daze, and certainly a birthday to remember.

On the way up to Oxford I hadn't mentioned anything about my special day, I had just been playing cards quietly like I always did, passing the time with Geoff, Herbie and Ronnie Rees.

But in all the excitement of the match I must have let slip to someone, because I remember everyone found out on the bus on the way back.

The manager stood up and said to the boys, 'Young Dai has done very well today. Not only has he scored four goals, but it's also his 21st birthday!'

Some of the press used to travel to the games with us, sitting at the front of the bus. As soon as they heard this they shot up to speak with me. That was definitely something extra for them to write about.

The rest of the players just said, 'You kept that bloody quiet.'

We travelled back to Swansea then, and that was that.

We might have stopped for a meal and a drink, but we did nothing special to celebrate really. I wasn't a big drinker back in them days as I would feel tipsy after just a glass or two of wine. Mind, I make up for it these days!

I did get a nice birthday present though, and one that I deserved – the match ball. I remember the first day back training after the game, probably the Monday, Len presented me with the match ball and the press were there to take photos of it.

I still have the photo, and the ball, which is safely up in my attic.

That was certainly not my last hat trick for Swansea. I was known for scoring quite a few in my time. In fact, in the FA Cup, I believe I am near the top in the list of players when it comes to the amount of hat-tricks scored in the competition.

I had a couple for Swansea, scoring hat-tricks against Telford and Rhyl in the following season's FA Cup. I know I also got one when I was with Halifax, and maybe Rotherham. I think I scored about five or six in the competition in total.

Winning against Oxford was our ticket into the third round, where we would face Leeds United at Elland Road about a month later. As FA Cup matches go, that was a dodgy old day.

Leeds were in their prime back then – a top First Division team, like Man City are today. That was my first time playing at Elland Road, and it was something we were all looking forward to because there was no pressure on us to come away with anything.

It was early January, and the weather in the week had been snowy and icy, so they had covered the pitch with straw to prevent it from freezing.

They sometimes used to light fires in big metal containers to keep the pitch warm too. They used to do that down the Vetch sometimes. They would never do that today!

But that day it was the straw they used, which was then raked off and piled around the side of the pitch before kick-off.

I always remember that because I wanted to get stuck in early on. So, within the first couple of minutes of the match, I barged big Jack Charlton and knocked him into the straw.

People used to say that he kept a little black book full of the names of the players who had wronged him on the pitch – those who he would give a kick to if he had a chance. I had definitely found my way into that book.

But I met him loads of times after that. I remember when I was at Rotherham United and he was manager of Sheffield Wednesday, he was always trying to sign me for them. He never did give me that kick!

That day we gave Leeds a hell of a game and quite a fright. We played really well and we went 1-0 up in the first half. Just like the previous game, I was the one who had scored for Swansea.

I can't remember the goal very well, but it was definitely scored with my feet from close range as opposed to heading it in.

It had gone from going up there hoping to give them a bit of a game to having thoughts of winning the match as we sat there at half-time.

We held on to our lead until well into the second half, but then things turned nasty.

Leeds were getting edgy because the game was getting on and they were still behind. At one stage I think Allan Clarke spat at Mel Nurse, so Mel went to grab hold of him, and the ref sent him off.

Sadly, down to ten men, we eventually conceded two goals late on. They had a controversial penalty awarded which gave them the equaliser, then Mick Jones scored the winner with ten minutes to go.

So, we were out of the cup, but it had been a decent run. I remember Don Revie used to come and watch a few of our games after that, probably because he liked what he had seen.

Overall, playing for the Swans was one of the best times of my career, bar the last couple of years.

After Roy Bentley left, Harry Gregg came in and changed the style at Swansea. He wanted us to bully the opposition more and wanted me to start kicking people, whereas I just wanted to play football. I still talk about it with Wyndham Evans now. Me and Wyndham always used to have to go up to Birmingham with Harry to have our disciplinary hearings for all our bookings and try to appeal or – more often than not – pay fines for the offences we had committed.

I remember we played Wrexham away and that was the last straw for me.

The ball came across and I was at the far post. I got to it and headed it back across the goal, but the keeper clattered me in the process.

When we came in at half-time, Harry said to me, 'David, never mind the ball – you should have knocked the bloody keeper through the back of the net!'

I said, 'What? I headed it down like I should be doing. Look, if you want me to do that, get someone else in to play for you.'

The dressing room went really quiet, with all the boys surprised at my outburst.

Anyway, the next week he made me captain of the side! That's the type of man he was. He appreciated somebody sticking up for themselves. But I didn't really like the way he played and that was it – I wanted to move on.

I had a few clubs interested in me but I went to speak with Halifax. I didn't have any intention of signing for them, but I decided we would go up there for a day out, myself, my wife, Ronnie Rees – who was experienced in that kind of thing – and my brother-in-law.

Those two went into town while my wife and I went to talk to the club. Before I went in, Ronnie told me, 'Ask for something stupid as a signing-on fee – and ask for £50 a week!'

Ask for £50 a week? That was silly money!

We went to speak with the chairman and the manager, George Mulhall, in a restaurant in a nice, secluded part of the town.

The chairman said to me, 'What are you looking for?'

'I'd need at least £20 more than I'm on at the Swans, and they are paying me top money,' I said. 'I want £50 a week, and two grand as a signing-on fee.'

He said, 'Give us a minute.' They went away and had a chat, then came back and said, 'Yeah, we'll sort that out for you.'

I didn't know what to do then.

To be honest, as we were driving up, I wasn't keen on the area. I thought, 'I could never live here – it's like something out of *Coronation Street*, with the cobblestones and terraced houses.'

It wasn't a bad area, but you forget how lucky you are in Swansea with the sea so close. In Halifax I had to take the missus up to Scarborough every Sunday just to show her the sea again!

But I wanted to move from Swansea and Halifax were giving me enough to buy a house, so it made sense.

On the way back home, Ronnie jumped into the car and said, 'How'd it go, mate?'

I said, 'They've given me what I asked for.'

'What!?' he said. He couldn't believe it. 'I've been to First Division sides and I've never had money like that in my life!'

I stayed with Halifax for a few seasons, then I went on to play for Rotherham.

Now, it's funny, but for all the goals I scored for Swansea, people tend to ask me more about the goals I scored *against* the club.

They always remember goals for other clubs, it's odd.

'Does anybody actually remember any of the goals he scored *for* Swansea?' my friends always joke.

A famous game that people always bring up was when I played for Rotherham against the Swans at the Vetch in 1978. I scored a hat-trick in the first half, and we were ahead 4-1 just after the break. But Swansea did very well to come back from that to draw the game 4-4.

In 1979, I left Rotherham to play for Newport. I had a nice couple of years there and we got to the quarter-finals of the [European] Cup Winners' Cup, which I think is the best any Welsh team ever did in that competition.

I had a great time at Newport, where we won promotion and we won the Welsh Cup. The Welsh Cup was quite important back then as it was a ticket into Europe. It would be Cardiff who used to win it all the time, so it was nice to win it for Newport.

I played my last league game for Newport at the age of 37, which was a hell of a good age in them days, especially for a striker who regularly got battered. Although I did play in midfield for Rotherham for a couple of years and became more of a target man than a scorer.

I still love watching some of the football today. Some of the skill and the speed of the modern game is fantastic, it's hard to keep up with it.

But the falling over puts me off.

That's the difference between our time and players today – the players today want to fall over at any given chance.

When I was playing, we used to try not to show we were hurt. I don't know how many times I broke my nose, but you try not to show it.

Having said that, I would have loved it in the box today.

JOHN TOSHACK: BORN 22 MARCH 1949, CARDIFF; 63 GAMES, 25 GOALS

John Toshack

Preston North End 1-3 Swansea City

Football League Second Division

Deepdale, 2 May 1981

After a prolific career with Liverpool, Welsh international striker John Toshack arrived at Swansea City in February 1978 as player-manager – he went on to change the club forever. At the age of just 28, Tosh's professionalism both on and off the field gave the Swans a platform to grow. Although he played just 63 league games for Swansea, he scored an impressive 25 goals – including the one that sent the club into the Second Division. As his career with Swansea went on, Tosh spent less time on the pitch and more time masterminding the club's rise through the leagues. In just four seasons, he took Swansea City from the basement division to the top flight, for the first time in the club's history. The famous day at Deepdale was one no Swans fan would forget and, even though he didn't play in the match, the legendary manager has great memories of the day.

Swansea City: Stewart, Evans, Hadziabdic, Robinson, Stevenson, Lewis, Curtis, L. James, R. James, Charles, Craig

Preston North End: Tunks, Taylor, Burns (Anderson), Haslegrave, Baxter, Blackley, Coleman, Bell, Elliott, Houston, Bruce

Swansea Scorers: L. James, Craig, Charles

Preston Scorer: Bruce

Referee: A. Challinor

Attendance: 18,970

51

WE REALISED as we went to Deepdale that this was the most important game – or at least one of the most important games – in the history of the football club.

Because it would mean Swansea going into the top flight for the first time in their history.

We had beaten David Pleat's Luton on the Tuesday or the Wednesday, which meant that we had to go to Preston to win to guarantee a place in the First Division.

Nobby Stiles was their manager at the time, the old Manchester United midfielder and World Cup winner with England. A lot of people nowadays won't remember that.

It was made even more complicated by the fact that Preston had to win to stay up. So, there was everything to play for.

When I looked at the side I was going to pick, the major problem I had was in that midfield area.

In my mind I pretty much had the team that I was going to play, but the doubt was over John Mahoney and Tommy Craig. Mahoney or Craig, Mahoney or Craig? This was one of the biggest decisions I ever had to make as a manager.

John Mahoney – Josh, as we called him – was a terrific professional and Welsh international, and, of course, he was my cousin. Tommy had a very cultured left foot, although perhaps not the all-round work-rate that Josh had.

I knew that I had to play the attacking trio of Leighton James, Alan Curtis and Jeremy Charles. And, of course, Robbie James in the midfield area, God bless him.

I tossed it over and over, and I eventually thought, 'If I have Jeremy, Curt and Leighton in attack, we might as well go all or nothing.'

Tommy was better equipped to give them the kind of passes that they needed than maybe Josh was. And I had Robbie who could do that extra work in the midfield area, alongside Tommy.

As a kid, I had played football with John Mahoney on the streets of Cardiff, when we were ten or 11 years of age. He was a second cousin of mine, and he used to come down on holiday from Manchester with his father, Joe.

I signed him in the belief that he would be a good buy, and just what we needed at that time in Swansea. Yet when it came to this final game, I just felt, 'Bloody hell, I've got a tricky one on here.'

I remember leaving this decision until the very last minute. The morning of the game, I think it was.

I had a chat with John on his own in the hotel, and I explained my decision to him. He was bitterly upset. Not angry or anything, just upset that he was going to miss such a vital game.

Then I remember going into the team meeting and explaining what I was doing, and I think a lot of them thought, 'Bloody hell, if he can leave his own cousin out of this match...'

That day, even without Josh, there were seven Welshmen in the side, which made us all that little bit prouder.

We were seven Welshman, plus two Scottish internationals in Tommy Craig and Dave Stewart in goal. There was also the Yugoslav Jimmy Hadziabdic at left-back, who became a firm favourite, and Neil Robinson at right-back.

I had signed Neil from Everton. He was a very popular player among all the lads. He was also a gritty little player – an aggressive type who brought things to the side.

He was almost like a young John Mahoney. In fact, I played him with John in midfield in some of the tougher games in the First Division away from home.

At the time of the Preston game we were playing the system that I introduced. People call it all sorts of things – 5-3-2, or 3-3-3-1, or whatever. But it was virtually shoring up the middle of defence and giving the two full-backs more licence to get forward.

That's the way it was, and that's the way it is now.

There are so many different takes on it. But what people forget is that the system depends very much on the players.

Honestly, I don't know what an 'attacking system' is, and I don't know what a 'defensive system' is. You can put a defensive system out with attacking players, or an attacking system out with defensive players.

A lot of people say, 'We're playing an attacking system – 4-3-3,' or whatever, but if your players are generally defensive types, then the system will be defensive.

Other people are playing it now, and supposedly introduced it, but we played this system almost 40 years ago at Swansea.

I stumbled across it because I wanted to play myself at centre-back. But I wasn't quick enough to play in a back four in those days.

So, I put myself in as a sweeper, behind a couple of young lads. Nigel Stevenson, first of all, and I think it was Dave Bruton or maybe even Wyndham, when we had the terrific result against Tottenham in the League Cup.

I have a little chuckle these days when I hear people talking about the modern system, but I know that I used this system for the first time ever at Swansea, and then I used it at Real Madrid.

That day at Preston we played that same system. The three defensive players in that system were Dudley Lewis, Wyndham Evans and Nigel Stevenson.

Now, they really were the heart of that team. Dudley went on to play for Wales, Nigel also went on to play for Wales, and Wyndham is as sound and as good a professional as Swansea City have ever had.

Wyndham was a Llanelli boy whose attitude in training and on the field during matches rubbed off on other people.

I want to mention those three – Dudley, Wyndham and Nigel – in particular, because very often they may be overlooked when we talk about Swansea racing to the top of the First Division.

But the true Swansea supporters with good memories should never ever forget those three. That was the heartbeat of the side that won at Preston.

We went out into the stadium that afternoon and the atmosphere was electric. The amount of people there from Swansea was incredible.

I didn't have to say anything to inspire the players, because everybody already knew the importance of this game. The fact that there were thousands and thousands of supporters from Swansea there, they didn't need any more motivation.

I was more concerned with getting it right tactically on the field.

'Let's go win it for Josh!' I remember that was the last thing I said to them before we went out on to the pitch.

These were experienced players, apart from maybe Dudley Lewis and Jeremy Charles, who were young lads. But there was experience in the team, with Leighton James, Tommy Craig, Robbie James and Dave Stewart. So, although there were some young players, there were players who knew what was wanted.

The game itself was full of action, and it took us just 20 minutes to open the scoring. It was a terrific goal from Leighton – a typical Leighton James goal. A run and a right-footed shot, which he curled in.

And then it was Tommy Craig who scored the second goal with his left foot a few minutes later. I think, in a nice way, that justified my choice to play him.

Then Preston pulled one back later in the second half through Alex Bruce.

In fact, I actually thought they had scored the equaliser soon after. I remember it being 2-1, and they had an attack. The ball came across and it was headed towards the goal, and from where I was standing I thought it had gone through the net! But it had actually gone just past the post. Dave Stewart gave a big sigh of relief. It was so close.

With everyone cheering and whistling, there was a sudden breakaway. Robbie James broke down the flank, and he played it to Curt who was out wide. Curt cut inside, then played it on to Charlo, who smashed it in.

Nine times out of ten that ball would have gone over the bar and out of the ground probably, but this time we were fortunate that it found the back of the net.

And that's how the attack finished. James, Curtis, Charles – goal.

People maybe don't realise, but for me that was significant. When I first arrived at Swansea a lot of people said to me, 'You've got three there – James, Curtis and Charles – who are too good for the Fourth Division.'

And it was those three that sealed the First Division for us.

When Jeremy scored that one we knew it was all over. The scenes after the game were fantastic. It was a terrific day all round, it really was.

I went to celebrate with Dudley Lewis as soon as the whistle blew. It was a terrific performance from Dudley.

Knowing him as I did, I could see that maybe in those last few minutes, before Charlo's goal, he was feeling the pressure a little bit more than anybody.

Because Preston had to come out, and had to get that second goal, so they were fighting for their lives.

I think, for a young boy, it was a huge, huge amount of pressure on him. I could see that in him.

Dudley was the youngest of all of them and he had come into the side at a difficult time. When Leighton Phillips was maybe not quite at his best, and I felt that I had to make a change. Putting Dudley in enabled me to keep the same system. Just change one for one.

It had been a great team effort and a terrific all-round achievement.

I remember Bill Shankly being there. Shanks played for Preston North End of course. He had played in the FA Cup Final for them at Wembley years and years before, when they won it.

I remember after the game, in the dressing room, he spoke the immortal lines to the BBC Wales camera crew, 'I think he's manager of the century – he's never forgotten what he's learned.'

To have Shanks in the dressing room gave the lads a hell of a lift as well.

We talk about Liverpool and Real Madrid, and I've been very fortunate as a player and manager winning championships, European Cups, FA Cups at Wembley; but if there's one thing that stands out for me, it was winning on that day.

Other times I've done things that maybe haven't been done before.

For example, Sociedad have only ever won the cup once in 1987, that was when we won against Atletico Madrid in Zaragoza. Or the record amount of goals for Madrid – 107, when we won the championship in 1990.

But this day, to take Swansea City into the First Division for the first time in their history, was a magical, magical day, and I would probably put that as the biggest and most satisfying memory that I have been fortunate enough to have experienced.

As exciting as the day was, I actually had no real desire to play.

When I had first come to the club, I had played in the Fourth Division, then I had played in the Third Division, and in some of the games in our first year in the Second Division.

But after three years, I realised there were other players who could perform over a period of time better than me. I was slowly easing my way out.

Of course, we also had good forward players there then, and when we got into the top flight we signed Bob Latchford.

I realised then that, at 32 years old, and with the injury I was struggling with, I probably wouldn't play much more. As a manager, you're watching games and there's other tasks to attend to during the week. Maybe you can't put the training in that you need to, to be able to play at that level.

I kept my player registration on, just in case, but, by the time we played Preston, I had more or less made the decision that that was it for me as a player.

As a manager, ambition was big for me. I remember Bill Shankly saying once, 'Consolidation should be struck out of the dictionary.'

I had come down from Liverpool and had these ambitions instilled into me – the old Liverpool way of thinking and doing things.

I just felt that getting to the First Division was what I wanted to set out to do.

When I went into management at Swansea, I felt I had to try to instil this same attitude into the players that I had.

But the big problem was – and this is what Harry Griffiths said to me when I arrived – 'When they play down the Vetch you can just sit in the dugout with a cigar in your mouth if you like. But once they cross that Severn Bridge, you've got problems.'

Back then, this was the Swansea thing. It was the reputation they had. Away from home, don't expect too much from them.

So, I said, 'Well, we're going to have to change that then Harry, because if we don't start to do it away from home as well, we ain't going to get anywhere!'

And slowly but surely, we did.

It was difficult, the old Vetch in the Fourth Division, as we didn't have the training facilities that we perhaps should have had. So that was the first step.

I mean, some days we trained on the beach, and we trained at Ashleigh Road whenever we could. We turned that around and got our own training ground at the old auto steelworks on Jersey Marine. That was the first thing.

Then we instilled little things like eating together. I got the players to sit in the old VPs' lounge at the Vetch after training and have a bit of lunch all together. Before that, it was only ever eggs or beans on toast, that Dolly used to do in the kitchen.

As we moved through the leagues we were able to do things a little bit more professionally – just things, to me, that were commonplace at Liverpool.

We couldn't do everything the way that Liverpool did, but we slowly managed to generally make the players feel a little bit more important.

I also remember when we moved up the divisions for the first time, Malcom Struel said to me, 'Welcome to the Third Division – you've got £50,000 to spend on players.'

So, I bought Alan Waddle for £20,000 – a good centre-forward who could ease the burden on me a little bit – and Geoff Crudgington, a goalkeeper, for £20,000. Those two positions are the most important if you think about it.

Then I gave Malcolm £10,000 back, and I said, 'Hang on to that, as we might need it in the transfer window.'

It makes me laugh now, when I think of what they're paying these days. Players earn more than that in a week now.

But that's what it was – £50,000 was the first amount of money I had to sign players to the club.

I think the two Yugoslavs I signed – Hadziabdic and Rajkovic – were a revelation, because at that time it was something new. I think Tottenham had signed Ardiles and Villa from Argentina around the same time, but signing foreign players wasn't as normal as it is now.

When you look at it now, the Swansea side are all foreign lads. I was recently talking to someone about the Liverpool side that we won the championship with. Myself and Joey Jones were the foreigners in that side, being Welshmen! The rest were all English.

Now you can't see an Englishman in sight – maybe just one or two.

Soon after the Preston game, Swansea had an open-topped bus parade around the city. Without trying to be too blasé, I've seen quite a few cities from the top of an open-top bus – San Sebastian, Madrid, Istanbul.

But the big thing about Swansea, was that it had never happened before. It was such a huge occasion, it really was amazing.

I remember saying to the lads, 'You've made history here – you've been part of the first ever Swansea City side to go into the top flight.'

Then of course, that first game in the First Division arrived, at home to Leeds, and that was another story to unfold.

ALAN CURTIS: BORN 16 APRIL 1954, PENTRE; 364 GAMES, 95 GOALS

Alan Curtis

Swansea City 5-1 Leeds United
Football League First Division
The Vetch, 29 August 1981

While the word legend is thrown around a little too easily these days, it's a title Alan Curtis wholeheartedly deserves for his work both on and off the field for Swansea City. Born in the Rhondda Valley, Alan joined Swansea as a youngster in the early 1970s and quickly became a pivotal part of the club's rise from the Fourth Division to the top flight. He was a clever and skilful forward, with no trouble finding the back of the net. Over three separate spells, the Welsh international made a total of 438 combined appearances for the Swans, scoring 123 goals in all competitions – firmly cementing himself as one of the club's greatest ever goalscorers. After his playing career ended, Alan returned to Swansea, taking on several back-room roles over the next few decades, including caretaker manager on several occasions.

Swansea City: Davies, Robinson, Irwin, Hadziabdic, Rajkovic, Mahoney, Curtis, R. James, L. James, Charles, Latchford

Leeds United: Lukic, Cherry, Hart, Greenhoff, Gray, Barnes, Hird, Flynn, Harris, Parlane, Graham

Swansea Scorers: Jeremy Charles, Bob Latchford (3), Alan Curtis

Leeds Scorer: Derek Parlane

Referee: S. Bates

Attendance: 23,489

TAKE away some of the international matches and there are two games that stand out for me in my career – the game against Preston North End at Deepdale in May 1981, where we won promotion to the First Division, and then the first game in the top flight against Leeds a few months later.

Preston was the opportunity to get into the top flight for the first time in the club's history – which was remarkable really, considering the amount of quality players we had produced over the decades, especially going back to the 1950s.

Tom Kiley, Cliffy Jones, Terry Medwin, Harry Griffiths, Mel Charles, Ivor Allchurch – what a team. The amazing thing is that if that team had got into the First Division, we would have been there for years and years.

These days I think the club's achievement of getting into the Premier League probably outweighs what we did in the 1980s, because it's so difficult to get there.

But that doesn't take away the fact that it was the club's first time ever in the First Division, going into a league that we had never played in before. Back then the top flight was still a tough league to get into.

I don't know if the standard was better, but it was an era when the English clubs actually dominated in Europe. Villa had won the European Cup, Liverpool had also won it, Ipswich had won the UEFA Cup, and Spurs had won the Cup Winners' Cup.

So, the Preston game is a favourite of mine, as it was historically so important.

But the Leeds game was important for me as an individual. It was our first game in the top flight, and – from a personal point of view – the fact that it was against Leeds, and the fact it was a home game, made it even more special.

It was the build-up as much as anything. The fixtures come out in the summer, and I think I was actually on holiday in Spain at the time. When they said we were going to play Leeds first there was almost a bit of disbelief from me.

I think there was a little bit of an edge to the pre-season training that year because we were going into the unknown.

Everybody looked forward to training that summer. Sometimes players would miss training if they had a niggle or a slight strain, but I think everybody really trained their hardest and looked after themselves during the summer in anticipation of the season we were about to embark on.

We actually went away as a team on the Friday night before the first game. We stayed in a hotel in Porthcawl called the Maid of Sker, which I don't think exists any more.

Tosh decided that we would go there on the Friday so everybody would be together. Stay overnight, have a meal together, get a good night's sleep, have some breakfast the following morning, then come in for the game. It actually worked out well, with the whole squad together, all refreshed. Then of course you would come into Fabian Way on the bus and hit a massive traffic jam!

The majority of them were Leeds supporters coming in for the game. Lots of them had got out of their cars and were walking around because it was such a hot day.

So, you have our team bus sitting there in traffic, and you have the Leeds United supporters banging on the bus – fairly good natured, but it backfired on them a little bit that day.

We got to the Vetch later than we had wanted and we were surrounded by all these Leeds supporters. Not the ideal start.

As we went into the changing rooms, I remember how nervous I was.

Everybody gets nerves before a game, but on that particular occasion – because of it being the first game in the First Division, the first game of the season, and a boiling hot day – I remember just before kick-off I was actually shaking a bit.

I remember thinking to myself, 'I've got to get a grip here.'

It's one of those things though. Everybody gets nervous, you're going back and forth to the toilet all the time; everybody is doing exactly the same thing.

The worst period for a footballer is that hour before kick-off, when everything is going through your mind. But I don't think I had ever been as nervous as that. Even my Welsh debut and debuts with different clubs – I think that day against Leeds was the most nervous I had ever been as a player.

But once you step out on to the pitch, you're back in control. You start to warm up, then once the whistle goes, the nerves drift away and you get into the adrenalin zone.

We actually started the game really well and we got the first goal, which is always crucial, especially in those circumstances.

It was the fifth minute. I remember I was going down the left-hand side of the pitch, and there was nothing really on. Leighton James played the ball down the line, I took it towards the corner and just put the ball into the box.

Jeremy got on to the end of it, there was a little bit of a deflection and it bobbled in, but it gave us a great start and whatever nerves we had were completely dispelled by then.

In any game, the opposition will always have a period of play when they are on top and to be fair to Leeds they got control of the game quite quickly, before equalising through the head of Derek Parlane after 26 minutes.

Then there was another incident in the first half when Carl Harris crossed the ball for their left-winger Arthur Graham, who had a great header at goal, but Dai Davies just managed to tip it on to the post and it came back into his arms.

Peter Barnes was making his debut for Leeds that day, and he also had a chance which hit the post and came back into Dai's hands, so we really could have gone in at half-time 2-1 down.

We always retained a threat because we had a bit of pace in the side. We had Robbie, Jeremy, Leighton, Bob and myself; all boys who could score goals. But we were glad to get in at half-time with the score being 1-1, because it would have been a different game had they gone in with the lead.

But then we came out in the second half and blew them away.

I honestly can't remember what Tosh said at half-time. I don't think it was that inspirational, it's just the way the game went.

Bob got his first goal as soon as the match restarted. The ball just dropped to him and he smashed it in with his left foot.

Then a couple of minutes later, Robbie – who tended to be involved in most of the goals – intercepted a long throw from their goalkeeper John Lukic. Leighton picked up the ball and he slid it to Neil Robinson in the box who crossed it to Bob Latchford, who was once again there to hit it in. That made it 3-1 and, all of a sudden, you've got a good cushion.

Soon after, I think I won a free kick out on the right, after being brought down. Leighton put a great ball into the box and again Bob Latchford got his head to it. It was his debut and he had scored with his left foot, right foot and his head.

I had played against Bob a few times before, and he was exactly what it said on the tin. You can compare him with Wilfried Bony – big legs, strong, and held the ball up well.

In the box, he was absolutely lethal. So, it was a great achievement to bring him on board, and he scored plenty of goals for us that season and the season that followed.

After Bob had scored his hat-trick, it was 4-1 and by then the game was won.

But I still had a point to prove.

The standard quote from everybody who plays against their old club is, 'It's just another game, there's nothing to prove, blah, blah, blah,' but you do want to do well and you want to beat them – and, ideally, you would love to score.

I loved to play on the North Bank side at the Vetch, as that was where you would really come to life as a player.

It was the 70th minute and Ante Rajkovic had got in front of Carl Harris and played the ball through to me, down the right near the halfway line.

People ask me, 'Did you know what you were going to do?' but under no circumstances do you know. It was one of those things that just developed.

The whole idea was to try to back the defender towards the goal. I think it was Trevor Cherry – who had been a team-mate just a couple of months previously. All of a sudden, he was backing and backing until he was almost on the edge of his own box. It all just sort of fell into place. In my mind it was almost done in slow motion. Back, back, drop the shoulder, then strike the ball as sweetly as I could and just try to hit the target. Thankfully it went into the top-right corner.

My celebrations were a bit exuberant and over the top – but defy anyone to celebrate that!

It was one of the best goals I ever scored, because of what it meant to me personally in terms of satisfaction.

I probably did score better technical goals in my career, but none that gave me as much satisfaction or sheer excitement as scoring that one. I can still watch it on television and get goosebumps!

I had a point to prove, although I certainly don't regret going to Leeds.

When I went there in May 1979, Leeds were one of the top two clubs in the First Division. It would be like one of the boys now going to one of the top two in the Premier League.

It's a huge club. I went up there recently as some of our loan players were there, and it's still a real fierce place to play, with a very partisan crowd. The atmosphere was exactly as I remember it – incredible.

But, unfortunately, injury played its part. I did my cruciate ligaments in January 1980 and I didn't come back until eight or nine months later – that took me a long time to recover from.

It was during the first half of a third-round FA Cup match against Forest. The ball had been played over their defence and it was between myself and Peter Shilton. He had come out to claim it, and I had got there a split second later. We collided and my momentum threw me over his body and I caught my knee. As soon as I did it I knew that it was a really bad one.

The swelling on my thigh was unbelievable – my leg was purple. But it took at least a week to try to get an operation on it.

That sort of wrecked it for me at Leeds, because by the time I was getting back to fitness we had changed manager. Jimmy Adamson, who had signed me, had been sacked and Allan Clarke, an ex-player, had taken over and he really wanted to bring his own people in.

I didn't really get to know Allan Clarke that much. I was just getting back to fitness when he was starting to implement his plan, so to speak.

I remember the first meeting we had with him as players, he said he wanted to be European champions within a couple of years – that was a bold statement.

Leeds were a fantastic team. But when you look at the honours board, you realise how many times they were runners-up in things – runners-up in the league, runners-up in the FA Cup finals. For the team that they were, they probably should have won a lot more.

In December 1980, I was back playing reserve football and thankfully the opportunity arose to re-join the Swans, who had been keeping tabs on my situation. Naturally, I jumped at the chance.

It was a chance to come back home, and it was also a chance to rebuild my career as well. Injury had taken its toll and I felt that coming back to familiar surroundings would have been beneficial, and thankfully it all worked out.

But I've stayed good friends and kept in touch with many of my Leeds team-mates. I've known Brian Flynn and Carl Harris for such a long time and we played together in the Welsh team. There were actually quite a few Welshmen in the Leeds team that day, including Byron Stevenson on the bench – who has unfortunately passed away.

I've kept in touch with others, like Eddie Gray who I class as a really good friend. He's still at Leeds. Then there's players like Trevor Cherry, Kevin Hird and Paul Hart – a lot of people you still see on the circuit.

It's always strange playing against former team-mates like I did that day. But it's one of those things. You put friendships aside during the game.

The game against Leeds was funny though. We knew we could give anybody trouble. I thought we were more than capable of winning the game, but I don't think we ever thought that we would turn them over 5-1.

We beat Brighton 2-1 straight after that, and you started to think, 'This league is actually okay.'

Then we went to West Brom and they beat us 4-1 – Cyrille Regis scored a hat-trick – and that brought us back down to earth a bit. But that game against Leeds will always stay with me as one of my favourites.

My professional playing career came to an end with the Swans in 1990, but then I did the rounds.

Not in any order, I went to Barry, then I went down to Carmarthen, Morriston, back to Barry – where we won the Welsh Cup against Cardiff in the 1994 final – Haverfordwest, Caerau in Maesteg, and I also played with Mumbles Rangers for a couple of seasons.

I only wanted to play with Mumbles in the thirds, so I could play with my two sons. Of course, then you would get people asking, 'Come and have a game with the first team,' which I didn't really want to do, but I ended up having a couple of games with them.

I tell everybody, play as long as you possibly can, because there comes a time when you can't do it.

It's great to see Trunds still playing. He's 41, but there's no reason he shouldn't carry on playing. He's certainly fit enough and skilful enough to keep on playing, so why not?

Around a year after I finished playing football, I took a community role with Swansea City. As the name suggests, Football in the Community was about taking the club into the community.

These days I think we have around 30 or so people working in the department, whereas you used to do it by yourself before.

It was basically going in to schools, working with the unemployed, special needs, women's football – anything which was out in the community. I even used to go to Swansea Prison one morning a week.

I did that community role for a couple of years, then I moved into looking after the youth team.

As for moving into management, there were a couple of times I thought about it – when the club seemed to lurch from crisis to crisis, and they were going through a dark spell.

In February 1996, Kevin Cullis was here for just a week before he was sacked. I remember thinking, 'This is a shambles.' Without actually applying for it, I considered giving management a go, rather than seeing the club continue down that road.

Thinking back, I was probably totally unprepared for it. But then Jan Molby was appointed and at least the club had a bit of credibility again.

I think I realised after a while that management wasn't really for me. I've always enjoyed the caretaker spells I've had, but I think it was always under the knowledge that they were going to be on a temporary basis.

I thoroughly enjoyed it, but I think you need to be a certain type of person to be a manager. I always felt my strengths were better as an assistant manager.

As a manager, you have to distance yourself from the players. But I've always enjoyed being with the players and having a little bit of banter.

You can't be too close to them, but close enough to put your arm around them when they come to see you with a problem. You're that link between the players and the manager. My forte was better there, rather than being the main man.

When it comes to being the caretaker, you can turn down the role, but you're not going to do that because the most important thing is the club itself. While the club is without somebody to steer the ship, somebody has to grab things and take control.

There were a couple of times you could see a change in management coming, because of results and speculation building up in the press. You can sense when things aren't going right, then prepare yourself for them to ask you again.

Paul Clement more or less came in straight away – within days – but when Garry Monk left, I don't think we had anything really sorted out, so I took over for a bit longer than I thought I would. Francesco Guidolin eventually came in, but then he was taken ill that time, so I had to go back in again.

But I think generally Swansea are a well-organised club. If there is going to be a change, the likely successor is already lined up.

I've had plenty of highlights over my career as a coach with Swansea and during my time I've gone through all the emotions.

I enjoyed being with the club in the lower leagues, working with players like Roger Freestone, Keith Walker, Mark Harris, Steve Jones, Michael Howard, Nick Cusack, Martin Thomas, Matthew Bound, Jason Smith and James Thomas.

They were great times, but scary times. Where we are today would never have happened if it had not been for the Hull game.

If we had been relegated in 2003, well, it doesn't bear thinking about.

Perhaps if we had have gone down into the Conference, the Liberty might not have been built. That stadium has been a big part of our success. As much as I loved the Vetch, it was time to move to the Liberty Stadium and to freshen things up.

Even though the Hull game was a horrible experience, there was an element of enjoyment over the fact that we came through.

I think before that, it was the lowest point for me.

The club had been in that position before – we had to apply for re-election when I was playing in 1975, when I first came into the team. But it was a closed shop, as nobody was ever going to vote to kick a League club out, as they may have been in the same position themselves one day.

But in 2003 we had to save ourselves. Thinking back, the Hull game was very scary and very emotional, but thankfully we got out of it. From there – after hitting rock bottom – we've just been on an upward curve.

I think this is probably the best time in the club's history.

People always ask me how the two teams – now and the early 1980s – compare. If you look at our team, we were together for a lot longer. These days the team changes almost every year. But if you took the best Swans team from the Premier League years, and they played the best Swans team from the first season in the First Division, it would be really close.

I suppose the difference is that the majority of the team in my day were local boys, whereas nowadays we don't see many Welshmen in the team. That's something that would be nice to see with the academy system. I'd love to see a couple more Welsh players.

But that's not to decry the foreign players, because they have all added some glamour and a touch of real quality to the club.

One of the best results we had in the Premier League was when Michu scored the two goals at Arsenal in December 2012. To be part of that was a fantastic experience. We've beaten just about everybody now and it's been great to watch.

I'm not in a coaching role with the club at the moment. You can never tell the future in any sport, especially football, but I don't envisage a time where I'll go back to coaching now.

It's actually funny, I tell people I've had a little bit of time off for good behaviour!

It's sometimes nice to go away and come back again. It's sometimes difficult to be there all the time. It's only when you leave that you appreciate how much you miss it and how big a part of your life it is.

At the moment, I am loan manager for the club. Wherever the players are going on loan they are being monitored by me, in terms of whether they are getting enough game time and whether they are enjoying their games and their training.

That applies to both the senior and the younger players.

I'm getting into the job now and I think it's quite an important role, because it's crucial that we monitor all the players to make sure they are progressing and that they are being looked after.

It's a role that has a fair bit of responsibility to it – it's not just a case of going to watch them play games and see how they are doing on the pitch.

There's a big emphasis on the welfare of the younger players. I'll look at their accommodation – have they got a nice place to stay? Are they eating properly? If they have their own apartment, are they able to cook? Because I'd be hopeless at that!

If the players are not playing games, why aren't they? I will speak to managers and coaches to find out how they are doing. I'll go around on a rota to see them play.

I am grateful to the club, because when I first came to Swansea as a 17-year-old, I never ever thought that I would still be a part of the setup at the age of 65, especially considering the changes the club has been through.

So, I feel very fortunate and privileged to have been a part of it.

Even though the last couple of years in the Premier League have been a little bit unsteady, I do feel the club is probably on a sounder footing now.

It's always going to be tough for us, because we're competing against the massive wealth of the other clubs, but we've shown that whenever we've needed results we somehow seem to find them.

The longer we're in the Premier League the more comfortable with it we'll become. I think we're in the position to kick on. I'm not saying the top six, but we can establish ourselves firmly into the middle table and keep that going.

For Swansea, I feel that there's still more to come.

LEIGHTON JAMES: BORN 16 FEBRUARY 1953, LOUGHOR; 88 GAMES, 27 GOALS

Leighton James

Liverpool 2-2 Swansea City
Football League First Division
Anfield, 3 October 1981

Welsh winger Leighton James had been a star for Burnley, QPR and Derby before joining Swansea City at the age of 27 in May 1980, for £130,000. His speed and eye for goal were a crucial part of the Swans' gameplan as they soared into the First Division under John Toshack. During Swansea's first season in the top flight he was the club's top scorer with 18 goals. After making 88 league appearances for Swansea over two seasons, he left to continue his career with Sunderland, Bury, Newport County and Burnley again, before retiring from professional football in 1989 – not before accruing 54 caps and ten goals for Wales. The passionate pundit truly earns his spot on the club's coveted Robbie James Wall of Fame.

Swansea City: Davies, Robinson, Irwin, Hadziabdic (Charles), Rajkovic, Mahoney, Curtis, R. James, L. James, Thompson, Latchford

Liverpool: Grobbelaar, Neal, Kennedy, Thompson, Lawrenson, Whelan, Dalglish, Lee, Johnson (Sheedy), McDermott, Souness

Swansea Scorers: Leighton James, Bob Latchford

Liverpool Scorer: Terry McDermott (2)

Referee: A. Challinor

Attendance: 48,645

FOR THE great Bill Shankly to pass away when he did, and us being the next visitors to Anfield – his spiritual home – you'd think somebody was writing this script somewhere and we were just part of it.

The previous season, as we were going up to the First Division, Bill had been at virtually every one of our games.

There was the obvious relationship between him and Tosh, but at that stage Bill had almost adopted us as his club. So, the link between him and Swansea was even closer.

People – myself included – had so much respect for what Bill had done at Liverpool. So, when he came to Swansea to support Tosh, even though indirectly, he was still a major influence.

A little word from Bill Shankly was something you took on board. You didn't think it was the ramblings of an old man. It was Bill Shankly and you'd be an idiot not to heed his advice.

The build-up to our match against Liverpool at Anfield on 3 October 1981 – the day after Bill's funeral – was almost surreal. There was a lot of newspaper talk about Tosh going back to Anfield as a visiting manager, being widely touted by many as the next Liverpool manager. On the blocks, so to speak. There was also an air, certainly in the national press, that we were just going there for Liverpool to celebrate the memory of Bill – we were almost lambs to the slaughter.

When you are a professional footballer, it's quite annoying when the talents of your team are pushed to one side.

I've always thought Liverpool have conducted themselves in the best possible way. But it seemed the football game was secondary that day. In fairness to Liverpool, they didn't create any of it – it was very much hyped up by the media.

It was all about Tosh and Liverpool, and strangely enough the one thing that fired us up even more was that Tosh was wearing a Liverpool shirt during the minute of silence – out of respect for Bill.

We realised that was all it was. But it still didn't go down too well in the playing ranks, I can assure you of that!

I think a lot of people perceived it as being an advert for him becoming the next Liverpool manager. We looked at him and thought, 'Who are you managing today? You're supposed to have one of our shirts on.'

But if you knew John, you knew he wouldn't have done it out of any disrespect for Swansea. It was out of total respect for Bill. We understood why he'd done it, but it still went a little bit against the grain.

So, before the game had even started, there was an element of, 'Right, we'll show you lot why we're here. We've not just come here to commemorate a great man, we've come to play a game of football – and we're intending to win.'

We were doing quite well at the time. We had started the season very well. We began with the win against Leeds, then we'd won at Brighton. We had suffered a couple of defeats, but by and large we'd had a very good start to the season for a newly promoted club.

I remember it vividly. The week building up to the match, the game itself was almost coincidental – 'Oh by the way guys, at three o'clock we've got a game to play, Liverpool against Swansea.'

Who cares about the game?

Well, two sets of players and 40,000-odd fans cared about the game.

I remember the match started quite well for us and we were quite comfortable. We attacked the Kop end in the first half. Liverpool used to do that – defend it in the first half, so they could attack it in the second half.

We settled very quickly. Saying that, we had a lot of players in our side that had played at Anfield several times, so the occasion of being there wasn't anything out of the ordinary.

In the 15th minute, Neil Robinson was brought down by Phil Thompson in their box – clear penalty. I was taking the penalties, so I put it on the spot and knocked it in the net, to the left past Bruce Grobbelaar; 1-0.

We got through to half-time with one or two scares, because Liverpool were a very, very good side. Bordering on one of the great sides I would say. Some of the players who played for Liverpool that day – Graeme Souness, Kenny Dalglish, and such – they would easily get into my greatest ever British team.

So, we got to half-time. I wouldn't say fairly comfortably, but we got there without too many major scares. Of course, we sat in the dressing room at half-time and it was, 'More of the same, lads.'

The second half started and, around ten minutes later, Bob Latchford knocked the second one in after a cross from Robinson.

Two-nil up at Anfield? That wasn't part of the script.

If Liverpool had lost to us that day, the reasons were already there for people to use. But as we know, Liverpool – being the side they were back then – came roaring back at us. In the 59th minute they were awarded two penalties in very quick succession, with Terry McDermott scoring them both to bring the game level.

The last 15 minutes were hair-raising at times, but we walked away with a share of the points.

Straight after the match I remember very vividly thinking, 'We should have won that game.' But, looking back, I would say that on the balance of play over the 90 minutes, we probably deserved a draw.

In reality, we were a little bit fortunate to hang on for a draw – if you looked at the last half-hour of the game, from us going 2-0 up, we were virtually hanging on by the coat-tails.

That result was still strange, because not many people in those days went to Anfield and got anything apart from a cup of tea and a good hiding!

I can just imagine Tosh's thoughts after the match were, 'Bill would have enjoyed that game.'

Because of Bill Shankly's more recent allegiance to us at Swansea, Toshack would have probably felt the draw was the ideal result for Bill. He wouldn't have wanted us to have lost 5-0 or something.

Two good sides he helped – Liverpool more so than Swansea – but he was still a big influence on Tosh, who was a big influence on our team.

The same season we played the return fixture, Liverpool at home, down the Vetch on a Tuesday night. On my birthday funnily enough, 16 February 1982.

We won 2-0. That night I scored the first goal, then Curt scored a goal that you'll never see the likes of again. He beat about five or six people on a mazy dribble from in his own half then slotted the ball past Grobbelar and you thought, 'My goodness, what a goal that was.'

But it rarely gets mentioned because Alan will always be remembered for his goal against Leeds, for obvious reasons.

That had been the third time we played Liverpool that season, because I remember around six weeks previously we had drawn them in the FA Cup and they had come down to the Vetch and beat us 4-0. Honestly, if we were still playing now we still wouldn't have scored against them! That was them at their very, very best – they murdered us.

But that 2-2 draw in October 1981 will always be remembered because of Bill and Tosh, and the weird build-up to it.

Strangely enough, a lot of the games that stick out for me have been between Swansea and Liverpool. There's been a subconscious link to Liverpool in my mind, because some of the best games I can remember have clearly been Swansea Town, or City, against Liverpool.

I've never really been an out-and-out Liverpool fan, but I've always been an admirer of them. I've admired the way that they've played. Bill Shankly, Bob Paisley, Joe Fagan – they were lovely people and great football men.

The first time I saw Liverpool play was at the Vetch in the old Second Division in March 1961, when Liverpool were beginning to build towards their greatest era. It was an evening game and we won 2-0. That's another one that sticks with me.

I was a Swansea Town supporter growing up. My first ever Swans game was when my dad took me down to the Vetch for the club's first game under floodlights. It was against Hibernian in October 1960 and we drew 4-4. Ever since then I've actually been a bit of a Hibs fan, as I used to like their kit!

I always remember watching the Swans as a kid. Along the pitch in front of the old North Bank, and the double decker stands behind the goals, there was a little red ash running track and little white painted walls, around 12 inches high, to mark the end of the track.

During matches the young ones were allowed to sit on the wall by the track. You'd get fathers passing kids over our heads, 'Young one coming over,' they would say. Little things like that stick in my mind. You'd never have that today, but we used to virtually sit on the pitch.

I never thought I would grow up to play for the Swans. Although even in those days I was ball-mad – football, rugby and cricket.

As kids we used to play outside my mum's house in Gorseinon. I remember the old concrete lampposts, which used to be triangular. The front used to be flat and the backs would come back to a point. In the winter, with the street lights on, that would be one of the goalposts, then in the summer it would be the cricket stumps.

I used to play in the back garden, kicking the ball against the wall, with my mum shouting, 'Will you stop doing that!'

Swansea City was – and it still is – my home town club, but I went to Burnley when I was 15 years old.

Some people say to me, 'Why did you go away when you were 15?'

I had gone away for obvious reasons. When I was 15, Swansea Town were in the Fourth Division. Burnley were a big club in those days, with probably the best youth policy of all. They came knocking on the door, Leeds came knocking on the door, and so did Birmingham – all First Division clubs in those days.

Swansea were in the doldrums of the old Fourth Division and not doing particularly well in that, until Tosh came down. It was very difficult not to look away from the lower divisions.

When I went to Burnley I was playing as a centre-half. I played in a trial match and my father was with me. Harry Potts was the manager, but Jimmy Adamson was first team coach at the time and he was at the game.

At the end of the match Jimmy came over to my dad.

'Mr James, we'd love to sign your son for this club,' he said. 'But I've got to tell you – if he signs for us while I'm involved with this club, he will never play centre-half.'

Ironically, I finished my career playing centre-half with them.

But at the time I just said – innocently because I was only 15 – 'Excuse me sir, why not?'

He said, 'Because centre-halves don't run with the ball and beat people like you can. It's just not the done thing. If you think I'm going to waste that running talent at centre-half you've got another thing coming!'

I had no concept of playing left-wing or outside-right, or anywhere other than centre-half. So, they shifted me to left-back, then pushed me forward to the wing. This is all within a couple of months, but the rest is history.

Over my career I played for Burnley at three separate times. It's a brilliant football club and a great little town. It will always be indelibly linked with me, and my career, and my life. I am very grateful for it.

They were very much the pioneers of what football clubs think is the norm today. Burnley were the first club to get its own training ground. They still have it to this day and it's still a magnificent thing to see now. It was down in the grounds of a stately home, Gawthorpe Hall – it was fantastic.

Their youth policy was great. They were one of the forerunners of the original youth system and they had won the FA Youth Cup two years before I joined, so it was a good time to be there.

But the chance to come back to Swansea ten or 12 years later was too good an opportunity to miss.

After my first spell with Burnley I played for Derby and QPR, but I was back with Burnley at the start of the 1979/80 season when Tosh signed me. We played against Swansea at the Vetch about early September. We had lost 2-1, but I had a very good game.

After that game I think Tosh spent more time on the phone to me for the next six months than he did his own family! He really wanted to sign me.

Burnley went down that year, so come the end of the season they said to me, 'We've had an offer from Swansea City, we're prepared to take it – do you want to go and talk to them?'

It was a long-standing transfer saga to say the least, from the beginning of October to the end of April.

When I eventually signed for the Swans from Burnley it was 1 May 1980. I played my first game in the last fixture of that season, against Charlton, which was after the transfer deadline. Not many people can say they had been played in a game having been transferred *after* the transfer deadline!

Tosh had been lining the deal up, but the transfer deadline had come and gone. So, Tosh phoned the league to see what could be done.

At that time, it was the one season that Swansea weren't involved in any promotion. They had gone from the Fourth to the Third, the Third to the Second, and it was the one season they were in consolidation – it's an awful word, but it was the one season they didn't have anything left to play for.

They couldn't go up and they couldn't go down, they were basically marooned in mid-table. Charlton were the same, virtually next to each other in the league.

So Tosh, in his wisdom, phoned the league and explained the situation with them, what he would like to do, and if it was all right. Because, apart from points, there was nothing to play for in that final game.

The league replied and told him, 'Phone Charlton to see if it was all right with them. Come back to us, and, as far as we're concerned, yeah you can play him.'

Charlton, in fairness to them, said yes with no objections.

So, I was a Swansea City player, ready to play in the last game of the season. Off we went to London on the train. We stayed in a hotel on the Friday night, then Tosh – as was his way – had a little meeting around 11 o'clock in the morning, to announce the team and so on.

He had already spoken to me before the meeting.

'Look,' he said, 'you've done a lot of travelling this week. Are you tired?'

'I am a little bit tired, but I'd still like to play.' But then I said to him, 'I'm fed up of wearing number 11, because everybody thinks I'm just a left-winger, but I think I'm better than just a left-winger!'

So, he said, 'That's okay, you won't be wearing number 11 today. You are number 12 – you're substitute.'

So, I was on the bench for my first game. But that's why for Swansea I wore number 9 instead of 11.

Anyway, at half-time we were losing 1-0 to Charlton. Tosh turned to me and said, 'Get warmed up, you're going on.'

'Who's coming off?' I asked.

'I don't know, but *somebody* is after that performance.'

As the second half started he took Alan Waddle off, and said to me, 'Go have a run around up front.'

Within 45 seconds of being on the pitch I had a ball knocked through to me, turned, ran past the centre-half and smashed it in the top corner. We won the game 2-1.

Walking off at the end, Terry Medwin, who was Tosh's assistant at the time – without knowing I was behind him listening – said to Tosh, 'Hey, I think we have a good one there!'

It was such a bizarre end to the season.

Tosh was very, very thorough in his planning, right down to the last detail. It might sound strange, but he was very superstitious.

He used to put the team sheet up on a piece of paper ripped from a notepad, and he would always put the squad up with surnames first, initials last:

Mahoney J.

James R.

Curtis A.

James L.

And so on. I had never seen anybody do it like that before, and that's always stuck in my mind too. But he was very, very thorough, so wherever we went we would know what the other team were going to do, and what we were expected to do.

For example, on an opposition corner, I would always be designated to be at the near post to attack the first ball in, because defensively I was quite a good header of the ball. But I couldn't score goals with my head. I scored about two in my life. One for the Swans and one for Burnley. I can remember them to this day. The Burnley goal was at Wolves away and the Swans was against Notts County at home, a 3-2 win.

I'll never forget it, because at the end of the game Tosh said, 'Well, I think I'll retire from football now – I've just seen Leighton James score with a header!'

When I look at my time at the Swans, I feel quite humbled by the list of players before me and after me that have represented the club. I feel quite privileged to be part of that list.

I played with some of the best of them. I was lucky. I played with Alan Curtis. Robbie James. Wyndham Evans. Nigel Stevenson. Bob Latchford. The two Yugoslavs, Rajkovic and Hadziabdic; imagine what those two would be worth today! All great players. I don't use the word great very often, or very loosely, but they were great players.

Not forgetting the ones that we had around them either. While they weren't as flamboyant or artistic, Tosh had blended a team that really complemented each other.

Hadziabdic and myself – people will still talk about that partnership. We didn't go on the training ground and say, 'Right, if you do that Jimmy, I'll do that, then you do that.' It was just one of those instinctive things.

I would look at him and think, 'I know what he's going to do here,' and he used to know what I was going to do.

When Jimmy used to run down the line, I used to know – without even talking – that he's got so far, he's not going to go any further, he's going to back-heel this.

And he knew that once he went past me, I would fill in at left-back for him, so when he used to back-heel the ball it would come straight to me.

People used to say, 'Oh, you lucky bugger.' No. We do this all the time in training. Monday morning he does it, Tuesday morning he does it, Wednesday morning he does it. This is how it works.

It was the same with Curt.

The first goal against Leeds United in August 1981 is a classic case of Curtis knowing what was going on.

The ball came to me on the left wing, and I was tight to the touchline. I couldn't get past. There was a big gap behind the right-back Kevin Hird and all I knew was that Curt was in the middle.

Curt was such an intelligent footballer. He knew I wasn't able to get anything out of the situation by beating somebody, and knew I would be aware that the space behind the defender was there for him to run into.

So, I just clipped the ball with the outside of my foot, up the line and Curt made the run, got the ball, crossed it and Jeremy Charles tapped it in the net.

That was our first goal in the First Division and it was all down to Alan Curtis's knowledge and ability to see the game, and to react to it.

And Robbie. What would he be worth today? He would be worth millions.

Because he could do everything. He could play centre-half, he could play full-back, and no doubt if you put him in a different colour shirt, he could have gone in goals as well!

He could play up front, he could play wide, he could play anywhere and he would still be a major force. A phenomenal player.

I've always said, of all the players in that side I was fortunate enough to play with, he would be the most expensive to buy in the current market. People would be clambering over each other to sign Robbie James.

He was four or five players rolled into one. He could score goals, could head a ball, could tackle. He wasn't the fastest, but over five or ten yards he was quick and strong.

Look at that team. I still think to this day that our 1981/82 team – that finished sixth in the top flight – is the best team that Swansea City or Town has ever had, in terms of the quality of players and the way we were allowed to play.

But most of it was down to Tosh because he was the leader. He was the ship's captain, and he knew who to pick and where to put them. He knew which size hand would fit into which size glove. He was very, very clever at that.

I've managed plenty of teams in my time, but I never enjoyed the managerial side of things. I always enjoyed the coaching side of it, but not the managerial side. I never really conformed to the theory that the chairman tells you this and you should do it.

No. If I walked into the chairman's place of work and told him how to do his job, the first thing he would say to me is, 'And what do you know about it?'

But they think, because they are chairmen with the money, that gives them the right to tell people about football. The chances are that the majority of people sitting in the stands, with ordinary jobs, probably know more about the game of football than some of these directors.

So, I've always struggled with that side of it, in terms of biting your lip and saying, 'Yes Mr Chairman, no Mr Chairman.'

Coaching-wise I've always loved that side of it, being out all day every day with the players – it was great.

But I've always been appreciative of what managers see. And Tosh had a great ability.

It makes me laugh when people talk about the Chelsea team in recent seasons and how Antonio Conte is a genius for playing three at the back – John Toshack was doing it in 1980! Three at the back is the most attacking system you can get. You can play 3-4-3 or 3-5-2. How many other teams played with three forwards? Not many. It's a successful system, providing you have got the right personnel.

We had a good goalkeeper in David Stewart. Then three centre-backs, Dudley Lewis, Wyndham Evans and Nigel Stevenson. Neil Robinson was a better player than people give him credit for and pushed in on the right, Hadziabdic on the left. John Mahoney or Tommy Craig in centre, and the great Robbie James on the other side. Then up front you had Alan, Jeremy Charles and myself.

Tosh worked it out and finely formulated who would play where, and it was very successful.

It's a system that others can't work out. If you play three up front you cause the opposition big problems, because they don't know exactly how many are up front, so they have to play four at the back.

The only time we had problems was when you played against teams who also put three up front. But not many teams were brave enough to match us man for man.

So, I do laugh at them sometimes. But that was a mark of how smart John Toshack was. He was a clever man and a brilliant coach, I have to give him credit for that.

The fact that Tosh was brave enough to do a Conte, 30 years before Conte was even thought of, just shows how good a manager he was – but that never gets mentioned.

WYNDHAM EVANS: BORN 19 MARCH 1951, LLANELLI; 389 GAMES, 15 GOALS

Wyndham Evans

Swansea City 0-0 Manchester United
Football League First Division
The Vetch, 18 December 1982

Wyndham Evans would be the first to admit that his autograph wasn't as hunted as an Alan Curtis or a Robbie James, but the Llanelli-born defender remains a true Swansea City legend due to his commitment to the club throughout the 1970s and beyond. A constant driving force at Swansea for 15 years, Wyndham accrued more than 400 appearances for the club in all competitions – one of only a handful to reach that impressive number. Tough and unyielding, the hard-tackling full-back joined Swansea in 1971 and played a key part in the team's defensive line, as the club rose from the Fourth Division to the First. He remained with the Swans as they dropped back down the pyramid, before leaving the club in 1985.

Swansea City: Davies, Stanley, Hadziabdic, Robinson, Evans, Rajkovic, Curtis (James L.), James R., Mahoney, Charles, Latchford

Manchester United: Bailey, Duxbury, Albiston, Moses, Moran, McQueen, Robson, Muhren, Stapleton, Whiteside, Coppell

Referee: T.G. Bune

Attendance: 15,748

THE MUNICH air crash. Thursday, 6 February 1958.

I remember listening to the news on the radio as a six-year-old in my bedroom. I was a big Manchester United fan growing up, which made it a very sad event for me.

Day by day, news was coming in that more people had died. Duncan Edwards was an outstanding young midfielder and was going to be the best player in the world, but he also died as a result of the disaster, which was tragic.

Thankfully Sir Bobby Charlton and Sir Matt Busby lived through it. I had fond memories of them, and I admired their desire to get back to the top when most of the team had been killed.

I never went to Old Trafford as a child, but I would watch United on TV whenever I could. The best game I've ever seen on television was in 1968 when they won the European Cup against Benfica at Wembley.

Law, Best and Charlton – those three were my favourites and so special to me. They were outstanding and played wonderful attacking football.

Denis Law was my hero and I used to write to him as a young boy. At the time there was a magazine called *Football Monthly*, and I would rip out the page with his photograph on and send it with a letter to Old Trafford. I would then get a letter back signed to me from the player, which was quite nice.

I never got to meet Denis Law, but I did meet Bobby Charlton when he played in the England XI for Herbie Williams's testimonial match in 1974. So, I met him and played against him, and I was quite proud of that.

I also got to play against George Best on 28 November 1975, when he made one of his comebacks. He was only around 29 when he finished at Manchester United, then he came back and played with a few different teams.

Stockport County offered him £2,000 a game, which was unbelievable money back then. His first game with them was at Edgeley Park against Swansea City.

In the days leading up to the game, all the press came down to Swansea to see who would be marking George Best.

Of course, it was me because he was left-winger and I was right-back. The press gathered around me, asking, 'What are you going to do to him?' I was just delighted to play against him, I told them.

When we got to the game we could hardly get near the ground on the coach, because so many Manchester United fans had come down just to see George Best. Women and girls everywhere, just screaming. People just wanted to see him play.

When I came up against him I couldn't believe how strong he was as an individual. Normally when I tackled people they would fall over and roll around, but he was as strong as me – if not stronger. He was so quick over the ground, it was like trying to mark a ghost. That's how difficult it was to get near him.

In the first five minutes Stockport had a corner and George Best took it. He curled it towards the goal and our goalkeeper tipped it over the bar. Then there was another corner and it came under the bar again, and we scrambled it away.

We all looked at each other and said, 'He's trying to score.'

The third corner came in and it was even better than the first two, right to the far post and there was a bit of a scramble before the ball dropped into the net.

I was marking him, but he was just standing by the corner flag, with his hands raised, as if to say 'I've scored.' I couldn't do anything about it.

He took three corners and eventually scored, that's how accurate he was.

I got to speak with him after the match. He actually came up to me because he knew I'd had a bit of stick from the press, because of my career record with regards to discipline. I think there was something in the papers that read 'The Beauty vs. The Beast'. Of course, I was the beast!

But I was just privileged to play on the same pitch as him. He was an absolute legend, although I feel a bit sorry for him really because he became the 'fifth Beatle' and such a superstar, he never got a spare minute to himself.

As well as United, I'd also been a Swans fan growing up. My father was a big Swans fan and used to take me to the Vetch as a young lad.

I went once with my dad and it was Liverpool at home in May 1962, when we beat them 4-2, just after they had won promotion back to the First Division. I just fell in love with the place and fell in love with Swansea.

My father was a local league footballer, although unfortunately he died at the age of 40, when I was 12.

When he died, I thought he was quite old. I always remember thinking, 'Will I get to 40?' And then when I got to 40 I remember thinking, 'God alive, he was young!'

He was a footballer, my brother played football, and I became a footballer as well. Football, rugby and cricket – they were the only sports you played as a child in them days, because it was cheap. Nobody had any money, so as long as you had a ball you could go out and have a game, it was wonderful.

I also enjoyed watching rugby and was a big Scarlets fan. I was there when they beat New Zealand at Stradey Park in October 1972.

I went to Llanelli Boys' Grammar School, and you were actually only allowed to play rugby. In fact, if you brought a football in it would be confiscated, which is crazy because loads of the boys enjoyed playing soccer. But that's why so many rugby players came through in the 1970s, because, in Welsh schools, rugby was dominant – there was no soccer at all.

In my later schooldays, we finally did get to play a soccer match against Dynevor Grammar School in Swansea. We ran out in rugby kits, because that's all we had.

In Swansea, soccer was massive, but we actually beat them 3-2. We knew how good we were because all the boys liked playing soccer, but the teachers were shocked because we'd beaten them!

As we were finishing school, soccer was eventually introduced. It's crazy that it was rugby-only for so long.

I left school and was playing senior Carmarthenshire League football. I even got into the Carmarthenshire League XI at the age of 16, which was quite young.

I was going back and forth to Stoke City at that time too, which I enjoyed enormously. But I wasn't going to become an apprentice at Stoke because my father had just died and I didn't want to leave home at that time.

Swansea got wind that I had been going to Stoke, so they signed me up and I played for two years as a semi-pro under Roy Saunders.

I had a friend called Dudley Morgan, who played for Swansea as well. We were both good mates, and we used to play one against one in the lane, tackling each other, hitting the ball against garage doors, kicking lumps out of each other. So, it's no coincidence that we both ended up playing for the Swans.

We played in the Football Combination, which was a fantastic league. Swansea were in the London Football Combination, so we played Arsenal, Chelsea, QPR, Fulham, Reading, and all the London teams.

It was brilliant, because we were in the Fourth Division with Swansea City, and we were playing against Chelsea reserves who were in the First Division. So, at times, the reserve players were playing against better quality players than those in the first team!

It brought us on quicker, because all of a sudden when you went into the first team it wasn't such a massive step up. You felt that, because you had played against Chelsea and Arsenal reserves, you could handle Bristol Rovers away.

It was a good upbringing, the Football Combination. There were no northern sides in the London Football Combination, so I had never encountered Manchester United in the flesh – until 18 December 1982, when we played them at the Vetch in our second season in the First Division.

It sticks out in my mind as one of my favourite games because I was such a big United fan growing up.

I had missed the games against them in our first season in the top flight. I hadn't really been in the team that season, but it got to May and we were down the bottom of the league and struggling defensively, so Tosh told me to come back in and play against Tottenham.

I was playing quite well in the game – my First Division debut – but then, after just 22 minutes, Spurs striker Mark Falco came across and hit my left knee. With a ligament injury, you know straight away that you've done something nasty.

That upset me because I was hoping to have a run in the team until the end of the season.

I eventually recovered from the injury, got myself fit and I was determined to come back. In our second season I played a number of games, and Manchester United was one of them.

It was a dry Saturday afternoon and the Vetch was packed. To have Manchester United, one of the biggest clubs in the world, down at the Vetch was wonderful.

I just loved looking at the team. I read Wyndham Evans, then looked at their midfield with Stephen Coppell, Bryan Robson, Remi Moses and Arnold Muhren, with Norman Whiteside and Frank Stapleton up front. That was a top-class team.

Being a fan, I used to know the strength of Manchester United teams and before the game I thought, 'God alive, how are we going to keep this lot out?'

They were second in the division at that point and on a five-game winning streak.

Myself and Jeremy Charles were playing at the back that day, with Jeremy marking Whiteside because he was quite a tall guy, while I was marking Stapleton. He was about my size, just a little bit taller.

Both teams had plenty of chances and quite early in the first half United thought they had put the ball over the line through Stapleton's head, but it was kept out by Bob Latchford.

Robbie James was playing centre-midfield that day and he had plenty of encounters with Bryan Robson. We were told to be wary of Robson, who was England captain at the time. A fantastic player who could score goals from anywhere, and he was extremely powerful.

That day, the tackling between Robbie James and Bryan Robson was some of the fiercest encounters I'd ever seen.

Two guys going head to head, banging away at each other. Bryan Robson had broken his leg twice, and he was still going flat out. But Robbie James was a wonderful player for us, a top-class guy.

We held out for the entire game, and we played really well. We nearly won right at the last minute, when Neil Robinson hit a great drive from 25 yards, and their goalkeeper, Gary Bailey, made a heck of a save to tip it over the crossbar. We were that close to beating them.

I went off pleased that it was 0-0 and that I had played against them.

Being a defender, I was delighted that Whiteside or Stapleton hadn't scored, and we had defended well, held out, and given as good as we got.

And as I say, we could have won the game in the latter stages.

It just felt special. Because I had played with Swansea in the Fourth Division – going to Halifax, Notts County, Rotherham and all those teams – I was pleased to play against Manchester United in the First Division.

In them days you didn't swap shirts with anyone. You had a new kit at the start of the season and that was it for the season. You had to look after your shirts.

But if I had swapped shirts, it would have definitely been with Frank Stapleton. I had stopped him from scoring and we'd had a good scrap.

I was around 5ft 10in – I would have loved to have been a bit taller, but I was strong enough to look after myself.

As I started with Swansea as a youngster, Herbie Williams was our captain and he was a good mentor. He was brilliant and used to be coaching me all the time while I was playing.

He always said to me, 'It's best to be in the bar at the end of the game and not the hospital.'

Everybody giggles about it, but it was such good advice. As a young lad going up for headers, I would be keen to win the ball, but people would be up there elbowing me.

I actually broke my nose three times in my first year and would always be in hospital having to have it straightened out.

Herbie told me to get my own elbows up into their face, rather than the other way around. He taught me how to look after myself.

Because, in the 1970s, both rugby and football were quite violent. There were no television cameras or TMOs, so you had to look after yourself.

If somebody kicked Alan Curtis, or kicked Robbie James, I'd say, 'Right, I'm going to kick one of them now.'

When Harry Griffiths was our trainer, he'd come on to treat Curt and then he would come on to treat Robbie, and he'd shout to me, 'Wyndham, I've been on twice – their trainer hasn't been on once yet!'

He felt like we were 2-0 down in that respect. In them days, if he had to come on again to treat three of our players, the opposition may have thought, 'These are easy meat, we can do what we like to these.' So, you had to fight back.

I had numerous bookings, and in my early years I was always back and forth to the Welsh FA, getting bans and I had a bit of a bad name.

But in them days if you didn't look after yourself or your team-mates – and I'm not saying Robbie James couldn't look after himself, because he could certainly look after himself – you would be taken advantage of.

I was an aggressive player. So much so that some people were trying to get me to calm down and take it easier with my tackling. I remember when Swansea signed Tommy Smith. He was a tough man and a very aggressive player. Smithy could hear what they were telling me. So, he said to me, 'Wyndham, you know all this calm down business? Bullshit. Get nastier. I guarantee that you'll be in the team all the time.'

And I thought, 'Thanks Tom, you're the only guy who has said that to me.'

But I could see him doing it as well, flattening people as he went in for a tackle. His advice worked because I was always in the team!

He was a character. I remember he got subbed off once by Tosh. Smithy was getting on a bit, but he still didn't like coming off the pitch. The following week we were playing away and Tosh played. He told Smithy to be the manager that day. 'Just sit on the bench and dictate what's going on,' he said.

Smithy said, 'Okay, Tosh, no problem.'

About 20 minutes of the game had gone by when Smithy stood on the touchline, holding up a number ten. He was taking Tosh off.

'What are you doing?' Tosh asked as he came off.

'Well you told me I'm the manager, so you're off. You pulled me off last week, I'm pulling you off this week!'

That's the type of guy he was though. If you got him, he would get you.

Guys like Smithy were tough, but they all had good attitudes when it came to training. The recipe for success is having good players first of all, but also having players with a good attitude. I'm a stickler for attitude.

When I've gone to coach kids, I can see immediately if somebody's got a poor attitude. 'What we doing this for, what we doing that for?' Just be quiet when you're training, and whatever coach tells you to do – do.

When Harry Griffiths was the manager, we used to come in on a Wednesday morning and run to the apple in Mumbles and back. Run from the Vetch, touch the apple, and run back.

It's exactly 13 miles. That's a half-marathon. Some of the players used to be crying coming in!

But I loved it, it didn't bother me. I was strong and fit, and a good trainer – I loved that side of it.

It wasn't every week, but when we didn't have a midweek game we used to do that. We would actually prefer a midweek game because we knew we didn't have to go down to the apple.

Roy Saunders would be there with the book, watching everyone touch the apple. It was good for your strength and fitness, but it was a total attitude test.

They were looking to see who actually wanted to do it, irrespective of whether you won the race or even came back, but that you tried to finish it and you didn't stop.

Smithy and Ian Callaghan had brilliant attitudes even in five-a-side games, they wanted to play and win all the time. They were two great lads.

When they came down it put a yard on everybody. In training, I just wanted to show Tommy Smith and Ian Callaghan how good I was, so it upped your game. Albeit, we had already put a yard on our game when Tosh came, and then when he signed Smith and Callaghan it just added another edge.

Tosh was keen for the club to move on when he arrived in 1978, and he played a big part in our success. It was a wonderful move by Malcolm Struel to bring him in.

We had scored 92 league goals the previous season, we were quite brilliant that year. We were getting more confident, so when Tosh came it was the icing on the cake.

He changed things at the club for the better.

For example, before then we were bringing our own training kit. You were handed your training kit on the first day of pre-season training, then you took it home and washed it and had to look after it, which was ridiculous for a professional footballer. Imagine if you'd left your shorts in the house or something like that!

These days it's all laid out for you, everything is perfect. Tosh created that at Swansea, he got us better kits and tracksuits, and the professionalism in the club went up.

When we heard there was a chance of him coming we didn't think he would actually come, because we were in the Fourth Division and he had played at the highest level with Liverpool. But then he came and he was in the team, which was great.

He came as a player-manager and was only around 29, but so confident. In our first meeting, he sat us down in the home dressing room, and he said, 'I'll have you lot in the First Division in three years.'

We all looked at each other, and thought, 'Christ, the confidence of the guy is unbelievable,' especially as we had been stuck in the Fourth Division for a couple of years.

He was close, because in the end it was four years – we went up from the Fourth straight away, up from the Third straight away, spent two years in the Second Division, and then up to the First.

So, it was incredible for him to say that, but confidence just oozed out of him.

Sadly, Harry Griffiths died just two games before our first promotion with Tosh in 1978. It was 25 April. As I came into the Vetch for training, Tosh said to me, 'Wyndham, Harry has died this morning.'

Harry had been like a dad to me, and I just couldn't take it in.

The big debate was that we were playing Scunthorpe in the evening, but Harry wouldn't have liked for us to cancel that game. He'd have said get on with it, as we were only two games from promotion.

So, we played and we won, then we won against Halifax on the Saturday as well and went up to the Third Division.

A lot of our success was down to Harry Griffiths, who was a top-class guy. He had formed much of the team from local boys like myself, Alan Curtis, Robbie James, Jeremy Charles and Nigel Stevenson.

Then you had Tosh who came in as a player-manager meaning that, all of a sudden, we had a top-class Welsh international and Liverpool centre-forward playing for the Swans, which was pretty good.

I remember playing with him for the first time. When the ball came to me and I didn't cross it into the box for him, he walked over and said, 'Wyndham, if you don't cross the next ball, you'll be off.'

He felt he could knock every ball in the net, as he was such a confident guy. He scored a number of goals before the end of the season, and he was a great player.

During our rise through the leagues he signed Tommy Smith, Ian Callaghan, Alan Waddle and Phil Boersma who were all Liverpool lads. So, you had a team of half Swansea boys, half Liverpool boys – it was hell of a team.

Sadly, things took a turn for the worse at the end of our second season in the First Division. We lost most of our games, and there was talk about money trouble.

Then the gate receipts went down alarmingly when we dropped to the Second Division, and we went on a bit of a downward spiral.

But that's football, it's all ups and downs.

My time with the Swans came to an end in 1983 and I left to play for Llanelli. I was doing well at Llanelli, we were top of the league and we had a good team, but then Tosh took me back a few months later, because I think they were struggling. He gave me another contract at Swansea, but then he got sacked.

Colin Appleton came in, then John Bond arrived in 1984. I was there as we dropped back down into the Fourth Division, then John Bond gave me a 'free transfer', which was unfortunate. They'll call you into the office and give you a free transfer – that's the sack.

But I went back to Llanelli as a player-manager, and Pembroke as a player-manager, then I went to Carmarthen as a manager when I had finished playing.

These days I'm still involved with the Swans and am down the Liberty Stadium hosting the '81 Club for every home game.

I just love chatting to the fans, and everybody wants to talk about days gone by.

I always ask everybody I meet there the same thing, 'What was your first game at the Vetch?' And everybody seems to remember vividly, it's great.

I was always a fans man, and I believe Swansea fans are the best in the world, whether you like it or not. I think they're so genuine.

I've been to away games at Rotherham on a Tuesday night in January, and you would get around 40 Swans supporters turning up.

We used to be allocated free tickets, so I used to get tickets from the boys and give them to those supporters, because nobody else was going to come up at that time.

As for me, I still love Manchester United now. I think when it's embedded into you as a young boy it always sticks with you. They will always be my favourite team – second to the Swans!

I love watching the Swans play Manchester United in the Premier League these days, but I always want the Swans to win, and we've beaten them a couple of times in recent seasons.

I don't mind a 0-0 draw, but I still prefer to beat them!

JOHN CORNFORTH: BORN 7 OCTOBER 1967, WHITLEY BAY; 149 GAMES, 16 GOALS

John Cornforth

Swansea City 1-1 Huddersfield Town

Football League Trophy Final

Wembley Stadium, 24 April 1994

Born just outside Newcastle in 1967, Super John Cornforth started his career at Sunderland before following Frank Burrows to Swansea in August 1991. A strong and clever midfielder, John quickly cemented himself as a crucial member of a successful Swansea City team. He was a great passer of the ball with good vision, and an authoritative leader, which is why he quickly became club captain. With an abundance of club pride, he played more than 150 games for the Swans in all competitions over five seasons – including leading his side to historic Wembley silverware in 1994's Autoglass Trophy – before leaving in March 1996 in a £350,000 move to Birmingham.

Swansea City: Freestone, Jenkins, Basham, Harris, Clode (Ford), Pascoe, Cornforth, Ampadu, Bowen, McFarlane, Hodge (Torpey)

Huddersfield Town: Francis, Billy, Mitchell, Scully, Cowan, Baldry, Robinson, Logan, Bullock (Dunn), Booth, Starbuck

Swansea Scorer: McFarlane

Huddersfield Scorer: Logan

Referee: J. Rushton

Attendance: 47,733

IMAGINE YOU are a player, and you had a checklist before a game.

'Do you want to play at Wembley with all your friends and family watching?' Tick.

'Do you want to captain your team?' Tick.

'Do you want to score?' Tick.

'Do you want to win the man of the match award?' Tick.

'Do you want to lift the trophy?' Tick.

After that glorious day in April 1994, there weren't that many boxes left for me to tick!

We had faced a mix of teams on the road to the Autoglass Trophy Final. Some we were expected to win – like the game against Port Vale at home – but there were a few potential banana skins too.

One of those was away against Plymouth on a wet and windy Tuesday night. Home Park is always a difficult place to go, and they had some good players who had played at higher levels.

But we went down there and from the word go we were brilliant. Andy McFarlane scored in the first half, and we went on to win 3-1.

I think it was that night, travelling back to Swansea on the coach, that I said to the lads, 'We're only a few games away from Wembley – this could be our year.'

And it was!

It's no surprise looking back, because at the time we had a great team. We had a strong base, with Roger in goal; Jon Ford or Mark Clode at left-back; Keith Walker and Mark Harris in the centre, then Steve Jenkins on the right. In midfield it was normally a rotation of myself, Colin Pascoe, Kwame Ampadu and Jason Bowen.

We also had Steve Torpey up front. On his day, he was as good as anyone attacking the ball, but he was a gentle giant. So, every game, Frank used to tell me to have a go at him and give him a kick up the backside to get him angry.

That was the basis of a good side, but most importantly we had a brilliant team spirit – the best I had experienced in my career.

After a hard week of training, which – if we didn't have a midweek game – usually peaked with a very tough session on a Wednesday, Frank used to give us Thursdays off.

So, we used to have a great night out in Sloanes on the Wednesday night – a couple of beers and a few glasses of wine.

That kind of thing promoted a great team spirit, because it meant we spent a lot of time together.

When you've got a good team spirit, with no massive individuals in the team, that transpires on to the pitch.

I thought that showed, especially during my era with the club.

I think Swansea had a lot to do with it too, as the city was a fantastic place to live. There were so many lovely restaurants and places for the lads to go. The fans too, they made it a great team to play for.

So, we had the recipe for success, especially with Frank in charge.

I played for some top managers in Lawrie McMenemy, Denis Smith, Barry Fry and John Gregory, but Frank was the best manager I ever worked under, by a country mile. He was a brilliant man and a brilliant manager.

I've known him since I was 16. I was a young kid at Sunderland, making my debut in 1985, when Frank was Len Ashurst's assistant.

All the way through my time there, Frank used to train us – he tried to toughen me up, kick lumps out of me, and teach me to tackle with some aggression.

I always remember going in for treatment one Sunday, just after I'd had my hair permed. Frank walked into the treatment room and caught sight of me.

His exact words were, 'Corny, I just got you fucking tackling, and now you come in looking like Shirley Temple!'

Frank moved to Swansea in 1991 and, soon after, I had a phone call saying that the Swans were offering 50 grand for me. It was a no-brainer. I drove all the way down to meet Frank, had a walk around the Vetch, and the rest is history.

He was the best manager I worked under, both on and off the field. He was as important in cultivating a solid team spirit.

He would have us doing different daft competitions in the dressing room, and then we would all go for pasta in a little Italian restaurant after training to refuel. This was well before other managers thought of doing this kind of thing. Genuinely, he was streets ahead of the rest. He was hard when he had to be, but he was honest and fair, and that's all we could have asked of him. I can honestly say my career wouldn't have been the same without Frank.

Getting to Wembley with Swansea was part of a whirlwind 18 months for me. It coincided with a lot of good things, such as getting my first Welsh cap.

Even though I was born in Whitley Bay – which is a seaside town around eight miles from Newcastle – I still qualified to play for Wales.

I always say it was because I owned five Bonnie Tyler records, but the truth is that I qualified because my grandmother on my dad's side was Welsh, born in Tonypandy.

I was in around eight or so Welsh squads, travelled to many different countries with the team, and ended up getting two caps – against Bulgaria and Georgia – before a knee ligament injury ended my international career.

But it was amazing being in those squads with some brilliant players like Ian Rush, Ryan Giggs, Dean Saunders, Neville Southall and Gary Speed, rest in peace. I loved every minute of it.

Anyway, that season we continued to do well in the Autoglass Trophy. After the games against Plymouth, Exeter and Port Vale, we faced Leyton Orient away.

It was a floodlit night down at Brisbane Road, and it was heaving there – not a free seat in the ground. Steve Torpey scored a great goal to put us into the two-legged Southern Section Final.

That would be against Wycombe – a future club of mine. First, we played them at home and beat them convincingly – it was 3-1 in the end.

When we went down to Adams Park we rode our luck a little bit, but thankfully Roger Freestone was outstanding in the game and, even though we lost 1-0, we got through.

And that was it – we were going to Wembley.

But we couldn't soak in the atmosphere as it was a busy, busy time for us. We were having quite a good run in the league and we were still in the Welsh Cup, so we had loads and loads of games to play.

Frank wasn't one to let us stop to think about Wembley. He would be watching in training, and if we didn't perform, we wouldn't play. Everything was high intensity, and that was the right way to be. He wouldn't let anybody go off the boil.

The build-up to the final was fantastic and there was a good buzz around the club and city.

We had a lot of attention from both local and national press and had things we had never seen before. I remember we had new tracksuits and new t-shirts, while Valsport got in touch with the club and wanted everyone to wear their boots.

Everyone did, apart from me, as I was the only player with my own sponsorship deal that I had with Mizuno.

I had been to Wembley a couple of times as a kid on school trips to watch the England schoolboys, and I'd played there once with Sunderland, as part of the Mercantile Credit Football Festival, which was a kind of knockout tournament that took place over a weekend in April 1988.

But going with Swansea was the first time I had been to Wembley for an official game.

Swansea is a massive club with a massive history, and to go to Wembley for the first time in the club's history was the stuff dreams are made of.

I remember travelling up the day before, we had some fun with our bus driver, Ken – as we always did.

Ken was a real character. He was about 80 years old. We used to have to shout at him on the bus as he always used to fall asleep at the wheel!

We'd always have a laugh and play some tricks on him.

Ken would shout up to us that he wanted me to make him a sandwich. The food on the bus back then wasn't like the a la carte meals they have today – it was just cheese, ham and pickle sandwiches that you put together yourself at the back of the bus.

'Corny – cheese and pickle!' He would shout.

So, I would make the sandwich and stick a couple of playing cards in there, so when he chewed it he would pull his false teeth out.

The night before Wembley, we were staying in a nice hotel near Watford. Ken was downstairs having a few pints of bitter with Frank and the staff.

With him occupied, me and Roger snuck up to Ken's room. We took all the legs off his bed, then balanced it on the loose legs. Then we put clingfilm over his toilet. We just caused havoc.

About ten o'clock, we heard him go up to his room. This was followed by a massive THUD!

The next morning at breakfast he came down and shouted at us. 'You bastards!' he said, 'I fell out of bed, and I have bruises all over my arms!'

But that was the kind of thing we did to pass the time and have a laugh. Ken was a great character, so he took it well.

The day before the final, we had been to Wembley to have a walk around. To walk out and see the size of the stadium was breathtaking.

The pitch was a bit bigger in diameter than the Vetch, and it was in good nick at the time. A lot of games were played at Wembley, but our match took place well before the play-offs and things like that had started, so we were quite fortunate.

The Vetch used to be a great pitch to play on too. Perhaps not when I first signed for Swansea in 1991 – back then the surface at the Vetch was awful.

But Frank used to ensure a lot of time was spent on the pitch. The groundsman, Dai Healey, used to do an amazing job, and worked day and night to get it ready.

Frank used to tell him what type of surface he wanted. Sometimes he would want the hosepipe out there as he wanted the pitch heavy, but, more often than not, he wanted it firm and level – we were a footballing side, who played our best game passing it around.

While Huddersfield had thousands and thousands of fans in London that day, all you could see as you came down Wembley Way on the coach was Swansea flags and the Swans supporters, singing all the Swansea songs – it was just something you never forget.

Despite the thousands watching, and all my friends and family there, I didn't feel particularly nervous.

I was never really one to get nervous before a game, which was a good thing as, being the captain, it was my job to have a chat with the others and make sure they were all right.

In particular, I remember Mark Clode was quite nervous that day, so I sat and had a laugh with him, and got him ready for the game.

It was also my job to go over what we had been doing in training and reiterate what Frank had said throughout the week – making sure everyone knew what we were doing in set pieces and making sure we were going out there as a unit.

I wasn't one for big warm-ups though. A lot of the lads wanted to get out on the pitch at two o'clock to warm up for a three o'clock kick-off – posing and smashing balls around the pitch.

I hated that.

I didn't want anyone out there until half-past two at the earliest. You only really need a 15- or 20-minute warm-up at the most, just to switch on and get ready for the game.

Even when I became a manager in later life, that was my pet hate. I didn't want the players out too early.

Anyway, we eventually got underway. The game itself was a little bit scrappy, and actually seemed to be over quite quickly.

The earliest incident I remember was that we had a free kick just outside our area after a foul, so Roger took it as the rest of us moved up the field.

He pinged a great ball up the field. I'm not sure if someone got a flick-on, but it ended up at the other end of the pitch with Andy Mac.

For weeks and weeks, we had been telling Andy to have a gamble in behind people, and that's exactly what he did.

He collected the ball behind the centre-half, touched it past the keeper with his chest, then put it into the far corner with a fantastic finish, putting us into the lead with just eight minutes on the clock.

We went crazy and jumped all over him. You couldn't blame us for going mental – we were ahead in a Wembley cup final!

But it was then a case of getting our shape back and getting the ball down, because Wembley is notorious for sapping people's energy.

We were ahead going into the break, but Huddersfield came out for the second half with some fight, and on the hour mark it was big Richard Logan – who I later played with at Scunthorpe – who scored a looping header from a corner.

So, it was 1-1 and that's how it would remain for the rest of the match. We had a few chances, but so did they. There was nothing to separate us and inevitably the match went to extra time.

That meant we had another half an hour to play. It was no worry for me, because I knew the lads were all fit – all Frank's teams were fit. But, as I mentioned, the Wembley turf was very energy-sapping and that would play a part.

As we prepared for extra time, I went around the lads to motivate them.

'If you're tired, you keep the ball,' I warned them. 'Don't give the ball away!'

And we kept the ball ever so well in extra time. In fact, I thought we handled extra time very well and dominated both halves.

But we just couldn't score and put the game to bed.

There were a few half-chances to win it. Jason Bowen had a canny chance that hit the outside of the post. Then we had a free kick on the edge of the box, with about three minutes to go.

I would take all the free kicks and for that one I bent it over the top of the wall beautifully. It was going straight into the top corner, but then Steve Francis made an unbelievable save to keep his side alive. I genuinely thought that was going in.

Huddersfield didn't have as many chances, although the few they had were kept out by Roger. He would smother anything that came in. Honestly, Roger was the best keeper in those leagues by a mile.

The final whistle went and that was that – the trophy would be settled by penalties.

But as soon as it went to penalties, I knew we had won it.

I just fancied our chances with our penalty takers, and I thought Roger was a far better keeper than their keeper. It felt a bit weird to be so positive.

We had practised penalties in the build-up to the match, but there's a difference in practising them at an empty training ground to taking them in front of 50,000 at Wembley.

Earlier that season, we had played Nuneaton in the FA Cup first round replay. We were losing 2-1 in extra time, although with about five minutes to go we were awarded a penalty.

I stepped up to take it and it turned out to be the worst penalty I had ever taken. I kicked the ground, it bounced around ten times, and the keeper caught it in his hat.

So that miss was playing on my mind a little, but at Wembley I just said, 'Lads, I'll take the first one.'

Huddersfield were up first. It was Graham Mitchell who took their first one and he hit the post, giving us the advantage.

As it pinged off the post, the ball rolled over to the Huddersfield fans. I went over to collect it and, of course, they were giving me plenty of stick. I always liked a bit of banter with the away fans, so I did a little Cruyff turn, flicked the ball up and caught it in my hands, just to wind them up.

I had a long walk back to the penalty spot, so I thought to myself, 'I'm going to give myself a long run-up, and I'm going to make sure I hit it cleanly and as hard as I can.'

And it was perfect.

Like when you hit a golf shot and the ball goes straight down the fairway, that's exactly how I hit it. It went straight in the top corner, and we were one up in the shoot-out.

Pat Scully scored for Huddersfield, then Kwame scored for us. They missed their next one, before Steve Torpey scored another for us.

That made it 3-1, and we knew that if they missed their last penalty, we had won the cup.

If you look at the video highlights, it's that moment that the camera pans to Frank on the sidelines and he shouts, 'Come on, Roger!'

It was their left-back Tom Cowan who would take the last one for them.

And it was the worst penalty I had ever seen. The kid kicked the ground and the ball bobbled, allowing Roger to stop it easily.

He had only taken a couple of steps' run-up and had no power behind it. The thing is, we were playing in front of 50,000 people, we had played 120 minutes, and your legs have gone.

He thought he was doing the right thing by taking a short run-up, but he just didn't connect with it.

I felt sorry for him afterwards, although at that moment it was all celebrations because we had just won at Wembley – it was unbelievable.

I had some great moments in my playing days, but that was the highlight of my career. I was also presented with the man of the match award, which was the icing on the cake.

For me to lead Swansea out on to Wembley for the first time in their history, to score a penalty, to be the man of the match, and to lift the trophy, it was just fairy-tale stuff.

After the match, we had to keep the celebrations low key. April was a busy time for us, and we had to play about four games in nine days.

We had been in the FA Cup, we had been in the Welsh Cup, we'd been in this competition, and we had a backlog of league fixtures to get through.

That didn't stop us heading to the suite at Wembley for a well-deserved drink though – plenty of beer and champagne was polished off that day.

On the bus back, Frank had the trophy and wouldn't let it out of his sight. He even moved his missus off the front seat of the coach so he could sit next to it on the way home!

However, typical Swansea, we didn't have any food left on the coach on the way back, so we stopped at Membury services to grab something to eat.

Of course, all the Swans fans had the same idea.

They just engulfed me, and I lost my Wembley jacket, my Wembley shirt and my Wembley tie. I ended up getting back on the bus in my underpants – the fans had taken it all!

I never went back to Wembley as a player, and only went back once more as a fan, to watch Swansea against Northampton in the Third Division play-off final in 1997. To be honest, I'm not a big watcher of football these days. I used to love going to games when I was a player and a manager, but since I'm no longer involved, I've lost interest.

The game has changed so much. These days I find it's quite boring, with a bunch of fairies and prima donnas playing – it does my head in!

My career with Swansea came to an end when Jan Molby came in. As I always tell people, Jan was a big bloke and he wanted to carry on playing, but there was only one big pair of shorts at the club – so he sold me!

To be totally honest, as Jan mentioned in his own book – called *Jan The Man: From Anfield to Vetch Field* – he couldn't physically keep me, because Birmingham came in and offered around £350,000 for me.

In that league, he needed the money to strengthen, so I ended up leaving Swansea and I was gutted.

A few seasons earlier I could have gone to Notts County, who also came in with big money for me, but I turned it down because I loved playing for Swansea. But this was the one time I had to leave.

I went to Birmingham, which ended up being a nightmare because it was Barry Fry who signed me, but he was sacked about three months later. Trevor Francis came in and bought loads and loads of new players, and I was just stuck in the reserves.

After that I went to Wycombe, with John Gregory, who was a very good manager, but I tore my Achilles in my first game and was out for eight months. So, that was another nightmare.

I eventually got back and played a few good seasons with Wycombe, scoring quite a few goals for them. But eventually, as I was the highest paid player at the club, they couldn't afford me anymore, so I had my first free transfer in 1999.

That's when I ended up going to Cardiff for a month, which was an absolute abortion.

Around 18 months earlier, Frank – who had left Swansea in 1995 and was now manager of Cardiff – called me at Wycombe. He said, 'John, come to Cardiff – Andy Legg and Jason Bowen are both here, I'm going to make you my captain, and we're going to win the league.'

I just said, 'Look Frank, I love you to bits, but I can't play for Cardiff.'

My wife at the time was from Swansea and my kids were born in Swansea, so I just couldn't bring myself to play for Cardiff.

They went on to win the league that season and, by turning them down then it probably cost me £40,000 in bonuses and things.

But it was a different situation when I had been given the free transfer. I was out of a job and I had no income coming in at all.

Frank called me again and told me to come down on a month-to-month contract. I had no choice – I had to join Cardiff.

My first game was Millwall at home, which ended up with riot police and police helicopters all over the place. They read the teams out and, as soon as my name was mentioned, both sets of fans booed. That was a good start.

I only scored once when I was at Cardiff, against QPR away in a penalty shoot-out. The fans were telling me to do the Ayatollah, but I refused. Because I refused, I was getting all sorts of threats.

Honestly, I had to get a police escort to my car at the end of every game, because you would have Cardiff fans waiting to jump me.

It was the longest month of my life.

I eventually became a manager for teams like Exeter and Torquay, but I came out of it completely in 2014.

These days I work for Cancer Research as the awareness manager in the north-east. I've done it for over six years, I work with a fantastic team of nurses, and I absolutely love it.

It's no stress at all, and you're not travelling the length of the country watching games, as I used to do when I was a manger.

I'll always remember my time with Swansea very fondly, especially that incredible day at Wembley. People still share the videos of the final with me on Facebook, and if I watch them I still get a tear in my eye.

From start to finish, I couldn't have wished for anything more.

MICHAEL HOWARD: BORN 2 DECEMBER 1978, BIRKENHEAD; 228 GAMES, 2 GOALS

Michael Howard

Swansea City 2-1 Cardiff City

Football League Third Division

The Vetch, 22 November 1998

Joining Swansea City from Tranmere Rovers as a teenager, Michael Howard soon made the left side of defence his own and became a staple of the Swans squad during the late nineties. Consistent and dependable, Howard slotted into a formidable defence that was the pride of the club for a few seasons, giving the Swans the confidence to beat clubs such as West Ham in the FA Cup in 1999, and winning the Third Division championship in 2000 – both games Howard played a big part in. While his final years with Swansea were a mixed bag, he contributed in the epic survival match against Hull City in 2003. Although he left for Morecambe in 2004, Howard eventually returned to Swansea to work for the Swans Community Trust.

Swansea City: Freestone, Jones, Howard, Cusack, Smith, Bound, Price, Thomas, Newhouse (Alsop), Watkin, Appleby

Cardiff City: Hallworth, Delaney, Ford, Mitchell, Young, Carpenter, Fowler, O'Sullivan, Williams (Allen), Nugent, Middleton

Swansea Scorers: Thomas, Bound

Cardiff Scorer: Williams

Referee: P. Taylor

Attendance: 7,757

I GREW up in Merseyside with a family split down the middle – my dad and my brother were Everton fans, while me and my mum were Liverpool.

So, I knew how intense a derby match could be.

My mum used to take me to the Kop as a kid, which was always great. You could stand in the stands back then, so the atmosphere used to be incredible.

We were also back in Europe in the early nineties after the ban, so there were some good European games there.

Even back then my brother used to come along with us – even though he supported Everton he just wanted to watch football. I didn't return the favour and go to Gwladys Street though, I always remind him of that.

I went to a few Merseyside derbies at Anfield too. It was different back then as you would get scatterings of Everton fans congregating in the Kop and the same with Liverpool fans in Gwladys Street. You would never get that now – it's completely segregated.

The Merseyside derby was always a great family occasion, and we'd always hate each other for 90 minutes. Even now, my brother won't speak to me for weeks after Liverpool play Everton, especially as they haven't won a derby for ages!

Growing up, Liverpool had a great team so I was always confident going into derby matches.

I used to idolise John Barnes. He was just head and shoulders above everybody on the pitch. Even in a really good side with the likes of Aldridge, Beardsley, McMahon and Hansen, it would be Barnes who would get you up on the edge of your seat. As soon as he'd get the ball, the whole stadium used to stand up in anticipation.

I was actually a schoolboy at Liverpool and was there from the ages of around nine to 16. That was a great time for me. Over the summer holidays I could go to Melwood and train, and all the first team players would be around you.

You would go to pick up your kit and bump into John Barnes or Steve Nicol – my footballing heroes. I was lucky to have access to the training ground like I did. When I look back, I think I took it for granted.

As I joined Swansea, I didn't know anything about the South Wales derby. To be honest, I didn't even know where Swansea was when I first came down.

At Tranmere I was playing alongside a centre-half called Andy Thorne, who had played with Alan Cork at Wimbledon. He told me that Corkie was looking for a left-sided defender at Swansea, and that I should push myself and go for it.

I didn't have an agent, so Andy rang my mum to ask if I was allowed to go down to Swansea for a trial. That's an example of how football has changed massively! Of course, she had no problem with it, and I was a mummy's boy, so it was my decision anyway.

I was only halfway through my first year as a pro. I had only played a handful of reserve games for Tranmere, which was actually quite a big thing back then as there were probably five left-backs ahead of me.

Anyway, Corkie had told us to come down on the Friday afternoon, so I drove down to Swansea in my dad's Maestro. But, as I turned up at the Vetch, nobody was there – the team had left for an away game.

So, I was down in South Wales with nowhere to go until I remembered that I had some distant family in Brynmawr, up in the Valleys. They were my granddad's side of the family, although I don't recall ever meeting them.

Still, as no one was at Swansea until the Monday, I drove up to Brynmawr, knocked on the door, and said, 'Hello – I've never met you, but can I stay the night?'

I eventually signed for Swansea in February 1998 and made my debut against Notts County as a sub at the end of the month.

After the season ended, I stayed in Swansea over the summer until the start of the 1998/99 season. Alan Cork was a stickler in training and wanted all the under-21 lads to come in two or three days a week over the summer.

The problem was that I was travelling down on the bus or the train from Liverpool specifically for training, then paying for digs on a Tuesday and Wednesday.

One day, Alan Curtis said to me, 'You're driving 200 miles to play for an hour on the beach!'

He was right, and it was tough. I was only on around £125 a week, so the cost of travel and accommodation was draining me.

Still, I had to do it because I wanted to make a good impression on the manager.

But, would you believe it, Corkie goes and gets himself sacked before the season even started!

I'd done all the pre-season work for him and he wasn't going to be there anymore. At that stage, I thought, 'I should have just stayed home this summer.'

I genuinely wasn't expecting to be in the first team the following season, but I had a good pre-season and the new manager, John Hollins, came in and put all his faith into me.

In fact, he gave me a new contract before I had even played a game.

'You're going to be my first-choice full-back,' he told me. 'I'll play you through your mistakes because you're 18 and I like what I see.'

I was thrilled. He sorted out my wages to bring me up to something more suitable for the first team, and he became like a father figure to me – he was fantastic.

As a club we started that season quite poorly overall, but we did well by the end, getting into the play-offs.

We weren't the greatest to watch, but we were a hard-working side and difficult to beat. Other teams would have seen us as a tough team to play against.

This was mainly because we had a good defence, so we didn't concede many goals, plus we had hard-working midfielders and strikers who put in the effort at the other end.

In fact, I'm sure it was only Cardiff that had a better defence than us that season, and they got promoted.

Talking about them, it was in November when the derby game against Cardiff took place at the Vetch. My first South Wales derby.

Most of the other boys drilled into me how important it was to win the game. We had a lot of Swansea boys in the team – Damien Lacey, Kristian O'Leary, Roger Freestone, Lee Jenkins, Jason Price, Jonathan Coates.

It was a good core of local lads who had experience of the South Wales derby, and they knew the importance of the match for the club and the supporters.

As November approached, all the players were aware the derby was coming up and wanted to be in the team for it. You would get players on the fringes of the team putting in more in training, and you would see a few more tackles going in.

I found the intensity in training picks up, as it does for most big games. Maybe it shouldn't be like that because, at the end of the day, it's just another league game. But you don't want to lose a big derby, especially as a player.

I lived near the town centre, so I didn't want to be going into the shop to buy the paper and bumping into fans having just lost to their greatest rivals!

For that game, I heard that neither Cyril the Swan nor Cardiff's mascot were allowed at the ground – probably to avoid winding up the crowd any more than they already were.

I can't remember who was playing Cyril at the time – it may have been Eddie the groundsman or Brian, who used to help sort the lads out with cars. He took over as Cyril after Eddie had the fight with Millwall's mascot.

Brian was very good for a laugh, but Eddie was bonkers. If it was Eddie at the time, I'm not surprised they excluded Cyril from the game – he was a massive Swans fan and would have been right up to the Cardiff fans, causing chaos.

Truth be told, the atmosphere that day was electric enough without the mascots.

Now, the build-up to the match is one thing, but when you are actually there and see the hatred in the fans' eyes, it's something else. You just know – *this* is a proper game.

People say the Merseyside derby is quite friendly, but I don't fully agree – I still think there's a lot of trouble around the city centre. But with the South

Wales derby I noticed straight away that there was more venom. It was much more of a fierce rivalry. It made it very interesting for me at 18 years old, and it was a good experience to play in one of those games.

Even though it was still a league game and still only three points up for grabs, the nerves were higher and we had to treat it like it was a cup match.

To be honest, I had to play like that throughout my career because I didn't have the greatest ability as a player.

If I didn't play at 100 per cent I probably would have been quite poor, because my 60 or 70 per cent wasn't good enough to play at that standard.

Players with great natural ability could probably cruise through games, but I had to give it my all. I always felt I had to play on the edge.

So, nerves were much higher before the game, but when the game starts and the tackles come flying in, you don't really think about it anymore.

If we were winning a game quite comfortably, like we did a couple of times, I could take a step back and take in the atmosphere.

But when the game is as tight as it was against Cardiff, it's hard to. You break your concentration for a second and you can give away a goal.

Sadly, that's what we did after just four minutes – we let John Williams put Cardiff ahead. That was rubbing salt in the wound, as John had played for the club a few years before.

I'm still mates with John and we talk about it now. He tells me it was an overhead scissor kick, but I'm sure he just volleyed it and it looped in over Roger. I'll take his word for it, but he is one to exaggerate on a story. Regardless, it was a good finish.

We were very, very poor for 45 minutes, and we should have been three or four down. Maybe the atmosphere got to us and maybe we froze, but Cardiff totally outplayed us. We were struggling and we couldn't get near the ball.

I was marking Mark Delaney and found it a tough ask, as they were creating lots of one-twos down the right in particular.

He was getting so much space, and John Williams was coming out wide, so I felt as if it was two-on-one all though the first half. We just couldn't get hold of their system.

We played 4-4-2, as was always the case with John Hollins in charge – he was a 4-4-2 man. I think Cardiff played 3-5-2 with wing-backs, and Kevin Nugent and John Williams up front.

They played the system really well and totally dominated the first half.

In goal, Roger made some great saves to keep us in it. He stopped a header and a close-range effort from Nugent, as well as a good shot from Jason Fowler. Stopping those gave us a chance to come out in the second half and turn things around.

As half-time came, we were really lucky to go in just 1-0 down. We knew we really had to up our game in the second half.

John made some tactical changes. Cardiff were dominating possession across the pitch, especially in midfield – we were overrun. So, he moved me up into midfield, pushing me on to Delaney to match their formation.

After John had his say in the dressing room, Alan Curtis took over. And, in my eyes, it was Curt's words that really changed the game.

The first thing Curt said to us was, 'Go out and have a fight.'

I would be interested to know if he said that to the Premier League players when he was in charge!

'Someone go and get a yellow card, go and get the crowd up, go and have a fight,' he said. 'Let's turn this into a proper derby.'

And that's exactly what we did.

We started the second half really well, with a couple of scuffles and hard tackles flying in, and we created more of a derby atmosphere.

In fact, John Williams went off injured because of me, and he still reminds me of it to this day.

We both went up for a challenge and I stamped on his arm on the way down, breaking his collarbone. He tells me I said some fruitful words to him as he was lying on the floor in agony, but I probably didn't say anything too bad.

I didn't realise we would become good friends when he came back to play for Swansea the season after we won the league, in 2001.

He's a great lad and I was really close to him. We still have a laugh about it, even though he calls me a horrible Scouse so and so for that challenge!

While we were two yards off the pace and couldn't get near them in the first half, we were matching them everywhere in the second.

We had some good chances early on and were closer to them all around the pitch. It had become a more even game.

They were still right in it though – we didn't completely dominate the second half, but we gave as good as we got.

Julian Alsop was subbed on around five minutes into the half, which also helped us. Jules was a good runner, you have to give him credit for how fit he was. He was also a handful for the opposition. He came on and bashed a few people around and worked hard as always.

We were missing that focal point in the first half, so it was good to have him as our target man and someone to hit the ball up to. Cardiff had three centre-halves and he just occupied them and helped us get further up the pitch.

In the 69th minute, our pressure finally paid off when Martin Thomas scored the equaliser. Jules headed the ball down and Tommo volleyed it in. No surprise, as he could finish two-footed. He had great technique and was always good for a couple of goals.

We needed that to be honest, because we never really scored that many.

Steve Watkin only scored about 17 that season, and Jules didn't score that many either. We just weren't a goalscoring team.

That's no slight on the strikers – we just weren't that creative as a team, so didn't give them much to work off.

We were more of a hard-working, two banks of four type of team. Which is why Tommo's goals were always invaluable when he chipped in with them.

As soon as he scored against Cardiff, the home crowd went mental and, from that point on, it seemed as if we were certain to go on to win the game.

As the match went on, there were a few goalmouth scrambles, but we just couldn't get a nick on the ball to put it away. We also had some other chances, and I remember big Jules had a header that hit the post at one stage.

But it was in the 88th minute that Matthew Bound blasted in the winning goal from a corner. For a defender, he was always good for a couple of goals too – cool under pressure and a good finisher.

After that it was just crazy. We just wanted to get the ball as high out of the stadium as we could to make sure we won the game.

But as soon as that one went in, we weren't going to lose.

I think we deserved the win for our second-half performance. Cardiff were a better footballing side than us at the time, but we had a bit more about us in terms of a never-say-die attitude.

We could dig in when we needed to and we'd certainly dug in that day.

It was an unbelievable feeling to win the first derby that you play in.

Admittedly, it wasn't a great game of football, but nobody really remembers how the game was played. It was a case of getting the three points and securing the bragging rights for another couple of months.

My parents were down for the game, and I took them down Wind Street to celebrate afterwards. I think we were out for three days after that. I don't think we got home until the Monday!

I remember on the Sunday, we all met in the Cross Keys quite early. There was a load of Swans fans in there and they were all singing Boundie's name. It was a great time and good craic.

When I look back on it now, I realise we had a big schedule of fixtures to play – we probably had a game on the Tuesday, but we were out celebrating like it was a cup final!

But we were all good mates, and that kind of thing helped me settle in at Swansea, especially being an 18-year-old living four hours away from home.

In the end I made more than 250 appearances for Swansea over the six seasons I was at the club and scored two goals.

I think I scored one in my first season, at Carlisle away – it was never a goal though. I took a free kick from about 25 yards out, it trickled through to the keeper, and he let it go through his legs. They all count though, don't they!

I also played in some big Swansea games of that era, like Hull, Rotherham and the FA Cup third round matches against West Ham – I have good memories of that fixture in particular.

It actually took place later that season, just a few months after the Cardiff game.

To play in such a big game – both home and away, in front of 26,000 people – having just turned 19 was a great experience. The international players they had, and the eventual result, was just fantastic for myself and the club.

Playing in the play-offs in my first season was also great, although losing to Scunthorpe at the end of the season still remains the biggest disappointment of my career.

I don't have many regrets in football, but losing that game is my biggest.

Scunthorpe were a decent side, but I can't believe we got knocked out by them. It was devastating. I would have loved to have played at the old Wembley, as that was the penultimate year the play-off finals would be held there.

In the first leg we absolutely dominated the home game, but I don't think we had many shots on target and – as I said earlier – that was our biggest problem. We really should have beaten Scunthorpe by two or three at home, but we only won 1-0 at the Vetch.

I remember Tony Bird missed a sitter which didn't help. He was one-on-one with the keeper, then I think he hit the post. He should have scored and that would have put us 2-0 up going into the second leg.

The second leg of the tie was a really heated match, especially towards the end.

As well as their striker getting a straight red card for a tackle on me, Scunthorpe were trying to waste time having gone ahead.

I remember arguing with Brian Laws towards the end of extra time. The ball had gone out of play and he was keeping it from me, so I was pushing and shoving him to get it back. He wasn't the nicest of guys at all, I really didn't like him.

It wasn't just me either.

My uncle was an Everton fan and a season ticket holder, but he gave up his season ticket to come down to watch me for most games.

He was down for the Scunthorpe match, and we couldn't get him back into the car afterwards – he was waiting outside the ground for Brian Laws to come out!

He was a big guy, my uncle, but luckily for Brian we managed to coax him back into the car!

As disappointing as it was, we hadn't been expected to get into the play-offs that year. But what we had been through in the play-offs helped form a really strong team spirit, and that was the start of our journey to promotion as champions the following season.

So, there were ups and downs.

Actually, I would say you can split my Swans career in half. I was there for six seasons – three seasons were good; three seasons were terrible.

The first three seasons I was being spoken of really highly, but the fans probably remember the last three seasons, possibly because it was so bad. We were really struggling, both on and off the pitch.

To be honest, I should have left the club when other teams wanted me.

After the Tony Petty period, when Nick Cusack was in charge, Stockport put three bids in for me. But I stayed with Swansea for whatever reason. I don't know why. I scratch my head thinking about it sometimes.

I played with some good players during my time with the Swans, but my favourite to play alongside would probably be Boundie. We had a good partnership and were well-known for being a solid defensive unit.

I was lucky because I was always first choice at left-back, with Jason Smith and Steve Jones vying for the right-back position. They would swap and change throughout the season.

To be honest, my form probably dipped when Boundie left in 2001. The centre-backs I played alongside after he went were nowhere near his standard.

We just complemented each other – I would cover him at the back because he wasn't the quickest, and he would win all the headers for me because I was a midget!

I always used to gauge my performances on what he'd tell me. If I had played well, he would tell me I had played well. If I had played poorly, he would tell me that too. He was more experienced, so I would listen to his opinions on my game.

I still keep in touch with many of the lads. As I said, we had a great team spirit, and that's probably why we were so successful.

We would travel away from home on those long journeys to Hartlepool and Darlington on a Tuesday night, and grind out 1-0 wins. We would defend well as a unit, so the opposition couldn't score against us, then we would nick a goal to win it.

I finished playing with Swansea in May 2004, then went part-time up at Morecambe for around six years.

My wife was from Swansea so eventually we came back down to settle the kids in school. With my football career behind me, I went off to college to get a training assessor qualification.

I was working in the town centre as an employability trainer, when the same role came up with the Swans Community Trust – the club's charitable arm. I put in for that and got the job. We get unemployed lads and girls back into employment. I've been doing it for three years now and I'm enjoying the role, it's very rewarding. However, because I still wear the Swans uniform, I think people assume I coach for the club, but I don't do any coaching at all.

I have done some coaching badges, but I'm not really interested in that side of things anymore. At the moment I take the Ynystawe under-10s and I love that too much – I would never give that up for another coaching job.

ROGER FREESTONE: BORN 19 AUGUST 1968, CAERLEON; 566 GAMES, 3 GOALS

Roger Freestone

Swansea City 1-0 West Ham United
FA Cup Third Round Replay
The Vetch, 13 January 1999

As Swansea City stalwarts go, it's hard to beat Roger Freestone. The charismatic goalkeeper spent a colourful 14 years with the Swans, and – with a total of more than 700 matches under his belt – he was the backbone of the club in the 1990s. After an earlier loan spell, Freestone joined the Swans from Chelsea in 1991 for a bargain £45,000, and quickly became first name on the team sheet due to his solid performances between the sticks and consistent reliability. In fact, he still holds the record for playing the most consecutive games for the club – 186 – between 1991 and 1994. His talent with the gloves was reflected in the 1999/2000 season, when he set another club record of 22 clean sheets in one season. He even contributed up the other end, scoring three league goals in his time with Swansea. Although he has little to do with football these days, Roger Freestone remains a true fans' favourite.

Swansea City: Freestone, Jones, Howard, Bound, Smith, Cusack, Coates, Thomas, Roberts, Alsop, Watkin

West Ham United: Hislop, Breacker (Hall), Dicks, Ruddock, Ferdinand, Lomas, Lampard, Sinclair, Lazaridis, Omoyinmi (Berkovic), Hartson

Swansea Scorer: Martin Thomas

Referee: S. Lodge

Attendance: 10,116

WHICHEVER way you look at it, I had made the club a lot of money by making that mistake.

It was in the 87th minute of our FA Cup third round tie at Upton Park, when Julian Dicks hit a low shot and it just squirmed under me. I was devastated.

Blimey, we would have happily taken a score draw before the match, but because we were that close to winning, the whole team was very disappointed it ended 1-1.

I think the only happy person in the dressing room was our chairman Steve Hamer. He was a lovely bloke – a real player's chairman. He was the kind of man who would come in and talk to us regularly. A lot of chairmen don't do that.

He was thrilled that the football club, as small as we were then, had come away with that result. It was a massive money-spinner.

Not only were we going to take half the receipts from Upton Park, but we would also go back to the Vetch for the replay with 10,000 people there. Money-wise, it was brilliant for the club.

It's not only the gate receipts from these games, but the add-ons. People buying stuff in the club shop, companies who want to sponsor the game, and all the extra revenue from that side of things.

When you're surviving on crowds of three or four thousand a week, it's really difficult for any lower league football team. These cup runs kept the smaller clubs going.

But that didn't really console me.

Going into the match against West Ham we had been written off by the media, but we had a good camaraderie in the team, so we were confident. We had some strong characters and some very good players, so why not?

I had actually hurt my hand a few days before that first match. It came from doing a bit of DIY work in the house. I can't remember what I was building, but one thing led to another, I got frustrated and punched a wall. Out of frustration and stupidity I suppose, but that's what happened.

I was in severe pain and was really struggling. Yet I didn't tell anybody at the club. Nobody at all, in case they didn't let me play in the big match.

It was tender and swollen, but I kept it to myself – no physios, no management, nobody.

I always remember we went up to London on the Friday and I was sharing a room with Steve Jones. I got one of those big champagne buckets from reception, filled it up with ice, and left my hand in there all night.

I strapped it up on the day of the match, but was thinking, 'I'm really going to struggle with this.'

It wasn't very comfortable at all, but I got through the game and it was fine in the end.

The atmosphere at Upton Park was fantastic before the match, and everything seemed to go well. We played well and Jason Smith put us ahead at the start of the second half.

But then, right at the end, Julian Dicks took that long shot that bobbled under me.

There was always an upset in the third round of the FA Cup and I thought maybe that was our one chance.

But there would always be another opportunity when we took them back to the Vetch. Nobody liked coming there with the hostile support that we had at the time.

We had just under two weeks to wait until the replay, but we didn't do anything special to prepare – just training as usual.

As the day arrived, so too did the bad weather. It was wet and windy – a horrible, horrible night for a match. We thought that would give us more of a chance.

Are they really going to fancy coming to the Vetch in these conditions?

The pitch wasn't the best, it was the middle of winter, there was a rainy, swirly wind, and a passionate support behind us. So, they'd *really* have to be up for it that night.

They had a good team with players like Shaka Hislop, Julian Dicks, John Hartson, Rio Ferdinand, Neil Ruddock and Frank Lampard.

We weren't that nervous facing them, it was just another game really, and that was the way we had to look at it. If you worry too much about things it doesn't help.

I rarely worried about games – I was more worried about being on the bench. I don't know why. Maybe it's because you can't control anything. When you're sat on the bench, you're basically helpless.

This is completely different, but I look back to when we went through the worries of relegation from the Football League in 2003. I had been injured but got myself fit again and I was sat on the bench while Neil Cutler was playing.

During that famous match against Hull City I was an absolute bag of nerves because I couldn't do anything to influence the game. But once you are playing, you know that destiny is in your own hands, in a sense. It's down to you.

Just as it was during the game at Upton Park. I made the mistake that resulted in the equaliser and that was down to me.

For the replay, the atmosphere was electric. But the crowd at the Vetch were always fantastic. Even for league nights, there was just something special about a dark evening at the Vetch under the floodlights.

There were more than 10,000 people in there that evening, and it was bouncing. When you come out and see the North Bank, and the reception you get off the supporters, it was absolutely fantastic and it just gives you that extra lift to do well.

Nobody probably fancied us to win that game, apart from those supporters – and ourselves.

Everybody else, in the studios and media, they would have said, 'Swansea have had their chance and West Ham will probably go there and turn them over.' But we were right up for it. I've watched the video of the highlights and we were really up for the game, and whether they were as up for it, I don't know.

Before the match, John Hollins was upbeat about our chances. Regardless of what game it was, he was always bubbly and chirpy. He was a fantastic manager. He had been at Chelsea, he had taken me there many years before that, so I knew him well.

So, when he came to Swansea, it was great for me because we'd had the Micky Adams and Alan Cork scenario at the time, with Kevin Cullis before that, so the club was a bit of a laughing stock.

When John came in he did things professionally and he had Curt on board too. That management team was wonderful.

John loved big nights like the West Ham game. He had managed at Chelsea, he had played at Chelsea, he had played at the highest level all his life, and he loved playing teams like that.

The weather was still awful as we approached kick-off, but it didn't bother me. When you first go out for your warm-up you may think, 'It's pretty windy tonight, those balls are going to be coming into the box quite erratically,' but then you forget about it during the game.

You are constantly running, jogging, keeping lively and organising your defence, so you don't really feel the effects of the weather.

As the match started, West Ham were on top, which we expected from the Premier League team. But we got into the game and we scored quite early through Tommo's volley.

Looking back at the goal, I'm not sure how it went in. It just seemed to go straight through Hislop.

I don't know if he was deceived by the wind or if there was a bend on the ball, but to get that early goal gave us a load of confidence. The crowd got behind us even more than they were already.

Then you start to think, 'It's 1-0 – is that going to be enough against a strong Premier League team?' Because it hadn't been enough two weeks before.

We kept plugging away, but West Ham had their chances too. Early on, Ferdinand headed just wide, but their first big chance came from Frank Lampard, who took a powerful shot from quite close in, but I pushed it out to my right for a corner.

Generally, we were comfortable, and as the game wore on we were happy to defend our lead. We actually had a few more chances to increase the lead, but we didn't take them.

As a game enters the last period, everybody becomes edgy. You're defending that lead. They continue to push forward. As I've said, on the pitch you're in control of it – in the stands and on the sidelines, people start to get a bit panicky.

The moment that stands out for me was the save I made right at the end. Neil Ruddock hit a shot from around 20 yards out, and I flung to my left and just got a really good hand on it.

It was fitting that it happened around the same time that I had made the mistake in the first game. It was nice to make up for that mistake.

But we still weren't safe. West Ham kept coming and I actually could have given them a penalty late on when I came out to collect a cross.

I've always said, as a goalkeeper, your shot-stopping comes naturally. It's the other aspects of your game that you need to work on, like how you come for crosses, your kicking and your distribution.

Most important, especially playing in the lower leagues, was the crossing. You had to be strong when coming for crosses. As I progressed through my career I got better. When I was at Newport County, many moons ago, that was probably the worst aspect of my game.

But as I grew and became more experienced, that was probably the strongest part of my game. I would come for crosses when I shouldn't have come for crosses.

I would like to think that probably eight or nine times out of ten I would get there, but you're not going to catch all of them – you are going to make mistakes.

And late on in the replay I made a big mistake.

I came out to collect a long cross put into the box and half caught it, but then let it slip behind me and I dropped it. John Hartson was there and he was about to hit it into the net, but I dragged him back.

It was a certain penalty. All the West Ham players appealed for it, but the ref said play on, and I got away with it.

We kept them out and when the final whistle went, it was a fantastic feeling. All the supporters invaded the pitch – there were thousands of them, all celebrating and congratulating us.

Then we had the joyous scenes in the dressing room after the game. It was like we had won the FA Cup.

To be honest, beating West Ham probably was our FA Cup Final. For a small club, as we were at that time, it was a great achievement for us.

I got a memento from the match – John Hartson's shirt. He's a big Swansea supporter, we all know that. I've known John for years and years, with the Welsh connection, but it was nice to have his shirt as a memory from the game. The only disappointment is that I didn't get it signed – I really should have.

We went on to lose against Derby at home in the next round ten days later, which was a bit of an anti-climax. Another rainy day if I recall.

You beat a Premier League team, then you think it would be nice to get another Premier League team. That's why we were happy to get Derby, but then we lost 1-0. We went out with a whimper.

It was a disappointing end to it all, but that was it. It was back to reality then.

These days, I think the FA Cup has lost its shine. When we were playing, it was the big thing. If we could get to the third round it was great as you always had the chance of getting a big club and we did. And it was a fantastic night.

I never really went out to celebrate games in those days. On the way home from an away game we used to have fish and chips, a few beers on the coach, and a bit of a sing-song, but I never really did much socialising with the boys.

Because I lived in Newport, I was sort of my own man. It was good to live out of the city, as you distanced yourself from everything.

I was close to Stevie Jones, and we had a good relationship – we roomed together, played golf together, and we would also drive down to the Vetch together.

There would always be a contingent of us driving down. Stevie used to come down from Bristol, so us two and Julian Alsop – or 'Big Stinky' as we used to call him – shared a car for a few years, and Jason Smith and Lee Jenkins came down with us for a while too.

We used to meet at High Cross, drop the cars off, then all jump in my company car and come down to Swansea. It was only an S-reg Mitsubishi Carisma by the way – it wasn't anything fancy!

But it was important that I had a company car, as I was driving back and forth to Swansea every day. Every time I signed a new contract with the Swans, I told them that I would sign for an extra 20 quid, as long as I got my company car.

All the boys used to jump in my car to travel down to the Vetch and back, and we used to stop off somewhere on the way home.

In fact, we probably celebrated the West Ham win with a hot dog and a bag of crisps from the Shell garage on Jersey Marine!

We used to stop in there every day after training to fill up with goodies for the drive home, so that was probably our celebration that evening.

It was a great time to be a footballer and it was a great time to be at the club. I have loads of good memories of my time at Swansea. Every day was a good memory.

It was a pleasure to go to work and spend time with the people connected to the club – the players, the staff, the tea ladies, everybody.

I used to go in to the club shop to see Myra and Joyce for a bit of toast and a cup of tea before games, and I used to actually serve fans behind the till as well.

I remember before evening games we used to train in the morning, then four or five of us used to go to Mel Nurse's hotel on the seafront in the afternoon. We didn't want to drive home and then travel back down to Swansea, so we used to grab a couple of hours' kip at Mel's, then he used to do us a bit of beans on toast pre-match.

It was fantastic – the camaraderie between the players, and everybody was close. Playing back then was fantastic. The fun we had, and the memories will live with you forever.

But then you had some dark days as well. You had the Kevin Cullis scenario. Absolute shambles. As I said, we were the laughing stock of the Football League.

Thankfully Doug Sharpe saw sense and took control of the club. He was fantastic for the football club and he did a lot for Swansea. He didn't get the credit he deserves.

Then you had Tony Petty. That was absolutely disastrous, and very scary because all he wanted to do was to milk every penny out of our football club.

Every penny that would come in on matchday would go straight into his pocket, which is why we weren't getting paid.

If it wasn't for people like Mel Nurse, Huw Jenkins, David Morgan and Nick Cusack – who was our PFA representative – then this club wouldn't exist anymore, because the man was hell-bent on just ruining the football club.

Colin Addison was in charge then, and I remember we trained Christmas Eve ahead of playing Exeter away on Boxing Day. We had found out we weren't getting paid, and he said to us, 'If any of you don't turn up for the coach, I wouldn't blame you one little bit.'

He even gave us Christmas Day off to spend with our families which was fantastic, because we usually trained on Christmas morning.

The next day, Matthew Bound was the only player who didn't turn up – everyone else was on the coach, and we won 3-0, which showed an absolutely astounding team spirit. We just wanted to show the supporters that Petty wasn't going to beat us.

It was around then that QPR were keen to sign me. But I didn't want to leave Swansea.

I remember being at a Halloween party at my friend's house at the top of the street, and every ten minutes I would get a phone call from someone at QPR. Every time the phone rang the offer would go up.

In the afternoon, the offer was £50,000 a year. I think the last offer was made around 11pm, and that was £156,000 a year. But I just kept turning it down.

They probably thought I was greedy or stupid. Probably stupid, because I wasn't greedy.

Me and Nick Cusack had a good relationship and I kept him informed of what was happening. The following morning, he came up to me and told me, 'You're fucking stupid – but I'm glad you're staying.'

He was right, it was a no-brainer really! But that was me showing loyalty and love for the football club.

If I would have gone I wouldn't have the same relationship with the supporters as I have now.

One thing that usually comes up when I chat with fans, and something I'm still proud of, is the fact that I scored a couple of goals for the club.

They were all under Frank Burrows. At the time, we'd had an absolute nightmare with penalties.

I think we'd missed five or six on the trot. So, I said to him, 'Gaffer, I'll take the next one.'

'All right son, you can take it,' he said.

Frank being Frank, I thought little of it. But soon after that, we played Oxford away and somebody went down. Penalty. I look over at the bench and Frank is there, gesturing to me.

'Go on, go on son,' and I'm thinking, 'Oh no.'

So up I strolled. I can still remember it vividly – smashing the ball and putting it right in the top corner. It was unstoppable. I just sort of stood there, then I started running around in circles. I didn't know what to do. Then everybody was jumping on me. What a feeling. Absolutely fantastic.

And that was it. We didn't have another penalty then for the rest of the season.

Then pre-season came along, and we were on tour in Cornwall, so we played somebody down there and we got another penalty. Everybody turned around to look at me, and I looked over at the bench, where Frank said, 'Go on.'

I took it, I scored, and that was it – I was the designated penalty taker.

For the manager to have the confidence in you to take a penalty was a good sign, but I just basically used to put the ball down and hit it as hard as I could.

I started practising them in training to some extent. I always put them to the keeper's right, low and hard, with pace on them.

In the first game of the new season we played Shrewsbury at home and I scored a penalty at the end of the game. Then two games later we played Chesterfield at the Vetch. There were a couple of thousand people in there on a beautiful, sunny day. We got to around 36 minutes and it was 0-0, then the ref's whistle went. Penalty.

I had the chance to put us in front. This time my heart is going crazy and my arse is making buttons. So up I went. I can still remember it now, walking up to the spot, wearing my pair of Mizunos.

I thought, 'Right, put it down, hit it low into the bottom-right corner.' Bang! I put it in. The noise was incredible. I remember running up the North Bank, just shouting 'Yeeeaaah!' It was such a feeling. The buzz you get from it was fantastic.

People would say, 'What if you miss?' But I had never really thought about that. If you missed you were in trouble. But I never missed. In the league I took three and scored three.

The only reason I stopped taking them was because Frank left and Jan Molby came in. Jan wanted to take penalties, corners, free kicks, goal kicks – he wanted to do everything. But I can proudly say that my record at Swansea City was took three, scored three. Although it's funny, because I've never seen replays of any of the penalties I've scored.

I broke some other club records – some of which still stand and some which have been broken since.

For example, I've been told that I hold the record for the most consecutive appearances for Swansea, with 186.

I also held the record for 22 clean sheets in one season, during 1999/00 when we won the Third Division title, but Dorus de Vries broke that in 2010 with 24.

I know I also had the record for the fewest goals conceded in a season, which was 30, also in that championship-winning season. That season I also kept eight clean sheets on the trot – that's another record.

While it's nice to hold certain records at the football club, as a person I don't really think about that anymore.

It was nice to play in the Alan Tate testimonial match recently [August 2017], and the reception I got was fantastic. To think, after all these years, that you are still fondly remembered is lovely. A lot of the supporters now weren't even born when I was playing – it was a long time ago.

When I left the club in 2004, I didn't really have a chance to say goodbye to the fans. The last game we played was York at the Vetch. I kind of had a feeling that I would be released after that, but I wasn't 100 per cent sure.

Nobody had mentioned anything before the game, but if I would have known maybe I could have given the fans a wave or something. So it was nice at Alan's testimonial to say goodbye properly and get a bit of closure.

I took my grandkids down to that match, and that was probably the first and last time they'll ever see me play football. When they are a little bit older it will be nice for them to look back at my achievements, my medals and my caps, and to think, 'Bampi was a somebody once.'

I never really wanted to continue working in football after I hung up my boots though. I wasn't interested in being a pundit or being a coach.

I did a couple of games for Radio Wales, but it just wasn't for me. I had spent 20 years being away on a Saturday, and it wasn't fair on my wife to keep doing that. Work all week, then go away to wherever I was needed on a Saturday, not getting back until eight or nine at night. It wasn't fair.

And I had no interest in coaching. Nothing whatsoever. I had lost a bit of my enthusiasm for the game. I got to a certain stage when Brian Flynn was there, then Kenny Jackett came in, and I knew my time was coming to an end.

When I left Swansea, I went to play for Newport County again, and one day I thought, 'What am I doing here?' I was at the end of my career and I just didn't want to play.

I remember I got injured playing in an FA Cup qualifying round game for Newport. I had really hurt my ankle. I had some injections on it, just so I could play a couple of games. But I thought, 'I don't want to be doing this. I just don't want to do it anymore.'

So I just retired. And I didn't have any self-doubt about retiring, it didn't affect me at all. It was just a case of you've done that, and you move on.

To me those days have gone now.

I'm a delivery driver now, I work for a company just down the road from my house, and it's ideal for me. I enjoy what I do, I enjoy meeting people, and I just moved on with life. And I'm happy.

I still keep up to date with the Swans, and I still go down to the Liberty, but I limit it to once or twice a year.

I'm looked after unbelievably well by the club – better now than I ever was as a player – and it's great to see familiar faces again, but I don't go down too often.

For me, that chapter is closed. Around 15 years ago I started a new chapter, and that is one that will continue until whenever.

MATTHEW BOUND: BORN 9 NOVEMBER 1972, MELKSHAM; 174 GAMES, 9 GOALS

Matthew Bound

Rotherham United 1-1 Swansea City
Football League Third Division
Millmoor, 6 May 2000

Born in Melksham in 1972, Matthew Bound cut his teeth in the youth system at Southampton, training and playing with the likes of Alan Shearer and Matt Le Tissier. However, it was at Swansea that he spent the happiest years of his career, joining from Stockport County in November 1997 and playing 174 league games for the Swans. He's remembered as a powerful centre-back who was a key part of a strong Swansea defence, while he popped up to score several important goals – many from the penalty spot. Although his career with the Swans saw several lows, he played a crucial role in some of the club's most glorious moments of the era, including beating West Ham United in the FA Cup third round replay at the Vetch in 1999, and then winning the Third Division title in 2000.

Swansea City: Freestone, Jones, Howard, Cusack, Bound, Coates, Thomas, Bird, O'Leary, Price, Boyd (Jenkins)

Rotherham United: Pollitt, Beech, Wilsterman, Hurst (Turner), Sedgwick (White), Branston, Warne, Watson, Thompson (Glover), Garner, Fortune-West

Swansea Scorer: Bound

Rotherham Scorer: Glover

Referee: R. Styles

Attendance: 10,863

AS THE ref blew up to end the match, the enormity of what we had achieved finally hit us.

It was the first time Swansea City had won a title since 1949. We were as elated as the fans and proud that we had added another accolade to the history of the club.

However, bizarrely enough, there didn't seem to be any real pressure on us to win the championship before the match. It certainly didn't get mentioned much in training. I'm not sure if that was a deliberate ploy by the manager to keep the pressure off.

I think because we had already been promoted to the Second Division the week before, when we beat Exeter 3-0 at the Vetch, it took a lot of the pressure off. The match against Rotherham was just a case of sealing the deal.

Whereas, if we hadn't been promoted, I think the pressure would have been massive at that point.

At the end of the previous season, we had missed out on promotion though the play-offs in the last minute of extra time up at Scunthorpe, and that feeling of desolation motivated us greatly. I think everybody sort of tuned in and thought, 'Next year, we have to go for it.'

Mentally, I think that genuinely helped us going forward.

But oddly, nobody really mentioned the fact that we were on the edge of the club's first championship title for 50 years.

We actually only needed a draw to win the title. Defensively we had a really good record. We didn't concede many goals, because everybody knew their jobs and everybody did those jobs well. So, we knew there was a very good chance that we would come away with at least a draw.

But in reality, we were going there for the win. We knew how many fans were going to be travelling up, so we wanted to win the match for them as much as us.

While the external pressure wasn't there, we certainly put pressure on ourselves to beat Rotherham. We were determined to not lose the match, and by not losing we knew we would win the championship.

The 1999/00 season had been fantastic. I think the reason we were so successful started with the fact that we had John Hollins as the gaffer, and he was very trusting of us.

I always remember bumping into him in Swansea a few years ago, and he told me, 'You do realise that I knew you lot were going out drinking quite a lot? But I let you get away with it because you looked after yourselves properly, and if anyone stepped out of line you would sort them out.'

He trusted us completely and gave us the freedom to express ourselves. It wasn't a free rein, because there were certain standards we had to meet, but training was good fun, and that kept morale up.

The seasons are tough – they're long, there's a lot of travelling, and there are plenty of those cold winter's days on the pitch. John used to let us have a bit of a laugh, as long as things were done properly, so that helped keep us on track.

We had such a good set of lads and as a group of players we were very tight knit. When I first moved down here we were all staying at the Glevdon B&B on Oystermouth Road. Because there were a few of us staying together, we had quite a close bond and we ended up taking that camaraderie on to the pitch.

It's a bit cliched to say, but when we were on the pitch, everybody battled for each other and everybody watched each other's backs.

Alongside Smudger for example, you would win a header and he would come over and smash you on the back and snarl 'good header!' and you'd all gee each other up.

And that kind of bred through the team.

Our biggest strength was defending – not just the defenders, but the team as a whole. If a ball came into the box, everyone would throw themselves at it. An opposing player had a shot, and you would throw yourself in front of it.

It was a brilliant feeling, every time you blocked a shot. The team spirit was so high. Real feel-good stuff.

So, we travelled up to Rotherham with great excitement ahead of the final game of the season, knowing that a draw would seal the trophy.

To add to the excitement, Rotherham were the only team that could steal the title off us – although they needed to beat us that day to win the championship. Ultimately, Rotherham were a good side, so we knew it was going to be a really tough game. But it was a nice twist actually.

I remember the previous week, after the Exeter match, we all went straight up to London for the PFA Awards.

At the awards, a few of the Rotherham players were there, and they knew we would be playing them the following week, so they were giving us a bit of abuse. But it was good-natured banter, there wasn't anything vicious in it.

We had quite a big rivalry with them – they were big units, and always gave us a great game.

Mike Pollitt, their keeper, in particular was giving it the big one. 'We're going to batter you next week,' he said. I don't know how many times they told us that they were going to win the championship.

So when we won the title the following week it was nice to shove it straight back down their throats!

We knew the sort of game it would be and it suited our style, because we were big lumps ourselves. So, it was a game we were all really looking forward to.

In the week leading up to the match we had a few injuries setting us back, with Jason Smith, Julian Alsop and Steve Watkin all out for the game. That was quite a big blow.

Smudger was like a rock in defence, and Jules – defensively and attacking-wise – was just a handful. He would go up for a header then you would see two defenders sprawled out on the pitch and you'd think, 'How's he done that?'

Steve was great at holding the ball up and bringing other players into the game.

So, they were big losses, although it speaks volume for the team spirit and the squad that we had that other guys were able to step in and do their jobs – and it worked.

For the Rotherham match, Kris O'Leary came in to replace Smudger. Kris was as hard a tackler as you would come across. When he tackled you, you knew it. I remember being tackled by him a couple of times in training – it felt like I had been run over by a truck.

He was as strong as an ox, and he was very good on the ball. Through his whole career at the Swans I felt he was very underrated. He was a great replacement.

Walter Boyd was also playing in that game and he was a decent player. To be honest, we didn't see a lot of him at Swansea because he was always too cold! He just used to sit in his flat with all his heaters on!

Walter didn't say a lot, but he was a nice guy. He was pretty small, but very lively, strong and hard to push off the ball.

While we kept quite calm in the build-up, the Swans fans were anything but. At the time, the internet wasn't really around like it is today, but there were these fan forums and notice boards which you would keep your eye on, so you knew the Swans fans were getting up for it!

We knew there was going to be a big following up there. I think the official number of Swansea supporters that day is said to be around 2,500, but I've spoken to loads of Swans fans who said they managed to get in without tickets.

Quite how they all got in there, I don't know, but it certainly felt as though there were more than 2,500 of them in there.

Of course, they made themselves heard – they were fantastic.

However, sadly there was a lot of violence between supporters before the match. As players, we didn't see any of it, but we were aware it was getting a bit naughty out there.

We were actually told pre-match not to do anything that might antagonise the fans, or cause a riot, because tension was already very high.

Then word got back to us about what had happened to Terry Coles. We didn't know his name at the time, but we knew a supporter had been trampled by a horse and was on his way to the hospital. But we didn't know he had died.

We were very aware of the crowds, although our main focus was on the game that was about to kick off.

Being played in May, it was a really hot day and Millmoor had an electric atmosphere. We could sense it before we got on to the pitch. For us to do that, we had to take a bit of an odd route, because there was some sort of work being done to the ground.

I seem to remember we had to get changed in temporary Portakabins, because the usual changing rooms weren't in use. Then we had to come down a path behind the stand – basically through a building site – to get on to the pitch. It was a bit surreal and that always sticks with me.

Eventually getting on to the pitch, the noise inside the ground was brilliant, as it always was in those old grounds. You just don't get that buzz nowadays – it's boring in some of these modern stadiums.

Oddly I seem to remember that the Chuckle Brothers were there at Millmoor, trying to get the fans going before the game – and the Swans fans slaughtered them! I might have the wrong game, but the Chuckle Brothers are Rotherham fans, so it would make sense.

Anyone who had been to that ground will remember the old Rotherham pitch was on a slope. Quite a big slope actually. These days it doesn't matter which way you kick, but Millmoor was actually one of those grounds that made you ask the question, 'Right, do we kick down the hill first half or down the hill second?'

As it turned out we played uphill in the first half, then down towards the Swans fans in the second. They were behind the goal at the bottom of the hill, and the noise they were making almost pushed you up the pitch! It really was that loud – like a wall of sound, it was great.

Now, I wouldn't say the first half of the match was a non-event, but it wasn't brilliant.

I don't think either team took the game by the scruff of the neck, and I don't think either created too many chances. I know we had one or two, because I remember their goalie had a very good game.

That afternoon I was marking Leo Fortune-West, and he was a proper handful. Around 6ft 4in or something like that. You know what his game is going to be – in the air. We all knew it was going to be a battle in the air that day.

I used to enjoy playing against him actually, because even though he was a strong, hard player, you knew what you were getting.

He wasn't going to beat you with fancy footwork or tricks, his game was about getting the ball into his chest or hitting it up for him to flick on. He wanted a tussle, so that he could try and bully you.

And we liked those sorts of games.

He had one or two chances himself, and he actually put the ball over the line in the 27th minute, but the ref disallowed it as there was a foul on Roger in the build-up.

But it was the second half when the game really came alive.

We had some good chances to take the lead earlier in the half, with Martin Thomas almost lobbing the keeper after I had set him up, but Pollitt did well to keep it out. He also stopped Jonathan Coates from putting one away.

Towards the end it started falling apart for Rotherham, who had two players sent off. Darren Garner was the first to go, for a second yellow, then Brian Wilsterman pushed the referee and was instantly sent off.

It got worse for them then because, with two minutes to go, we were awarded a penalty and had a chance to go ahead.

Jason Price had been taken down over on the right-hand side of the box I believe. It was so soft, I remember saying to one of their players, 'I can't believe he's given a penalty for that.' Don't get me wrong – we were overjoyed that the ref had given a penalty, but it was a dubious one to say the least.

I was designated penalty taker for Swansea at the time. I think generally, as defenders, you don't overthink things too much – you just get on with it.

I think a lot of forwards don't take penalties, when they clearly have the ability. They get so caught up in their own thoughts that they end up worrying about missing more than thinking about scoring. A defender will tend to just put the ball down and go, 'Right, this is what I'm going to do. If he saves it, he saves it – if he doesn't, it's a goal.'

That was my thought process anyway, and the manager was happy to go along with it.

So, the focus was suddenly on me. I put the ball down on the spot and thought, 'Don't slip up, don't trip over it, don't miss the target. Score.'

You could see the Swans fans were literally spilling over the barrier before I had even taken it, so it was like, 'If I miss here, I'm dead.'

I just wanted to run up, smash it high down the middle, knowing that if the keeper dived he wouldn't save it.

As it turns out, that's exactly what happened.

Pollitt dived and the ball went straight down the middle, at which point I made a mistake – I actually ran towards the Swans fans. I quickly realised they were all over the barrier, running towards me and I didn't have time to get away.

They all just piled on top of me to celebrate. It was hilarious getting engulfed by all those fans.

It was all good-natured at that point, but just after we scored the game was halted because there was a big pitch invasion. The police horses came on to the pitch, and that's when the whole afternoon just turned into mayhem. When it calmed down and we got back to the game, Rotherham were given a penalty of their own. I remember Jonah fouling the guy and thinking, 'Stay on your feet.'

However, theirs probably was a penalty. Of course, it felt soft to us, but it was probably more of a penalty than ours had been.

Before they could take it, we had the second pitch invasion and it was carnage for about 20 minutes.

As a player in these situations you have to just keep your wits about you. You're always looking around, making sure no one is going to walk up and have a dig at you.

Eventually we were taken into the changing rooms by the ref until they could restore order, because it wasn't safe out on the pitch. We probably sat in there for about ten minutes, with the gaffer telling us to think about the game and keep focused, as we had another couple of minutes to see out.

It can definitely ruin the flow of the game, although for us as players it was part of the theatre of it.

You're taking it all in, thinking, 'This is bonkers,' and you are almost enjoying it. Because, from a Swans point of view, it was fairly good-natured.

Of course, there was a bit of goading and a bit of aggression, especially following what had happened before the game but, as players, we just soaked it all up. I guess it goes against what I said about staying focused, but it's hard to help it sometimes. It's a bit of an adrenalin rush.

Eventually we got back to the match, and Lee Glover put away their penalty to take it to 1-1.

We were a bit gutted after that, because up until then we had been comfortable. To give them an opportunity to get back in the game when the game should have been dead – them down to nine men, us one goal up, the last few minutes – that was frustrating.

The final minutes, including injury time, were complete carnage. The ref lost all control of the game by that point. Loads of fouls, and people pushing each other over, here, there and everywhere.

Rotherham still needed the second goal and they bombarded the box. We were pretty much just camped out in our six-yard box.

Two of us were stood next to Fortune-West, just trying to stop him heading anything and trying to stop him moving effectively. Because if he got any touch on it, he could cause chaos.

They had one or two chances towards the end, but we dug in and got through it.

The feeling of elation when we did win was great. There was certainly a bit of relief after such a long season and a testing final game, but it was mainly joy as we realised the enormity of it.

It was also so nice to see the reaction of the fans and what it meant to everyone associated with Swansea.

After the match, there was a presentation on the pitch, up at the halfway line. I actually can't remember if we had the trophy or not, but we certainly had medals presented on the day.

Of course, our celebrations were a bit muted because, when we returned to the changing rooms, the gaffer broke the news to us that Terry Coles had passed away.

That was surreal to hear actually. You start thinking, 'That guy left his house at six o'clock this morning to go and watch a football game, and now he's dead.'

It put the day in perspective.

It was just a horrible thing to be involved with, and we were involved with it because, ultimately, he was coming to watch us play. Although we didn't feel responsible, we felt really, really deflated.

The gaffer said, 'Look guys, the celebrations have been cancelled, out of respect for the supporter.'

We had a couple of beers on the bus on the way back to Swansea but stayed respectful. And that was pretty much the end of it.

We had a really good bond with the fans, and the day at Rotherham made that bond even stronger.

It was just such a shame what happened to Terry because it would have been a fitting end to the season for all the lads to go out with the fans that night.

But all round, apart from the violence, the whole day was brilliant.

In fact, my entire career with Swansea was brilliant. Overall, I loved every minute of it. It was definitely topsy-turvy in terms of promotion and relegation, and all the stuff that went on off the pitch. There was always a drama of some sort, and it was generally a big learning curve.

But I really enjoyed it and made some really good friends. I've still also got some Swans fans who are my friends, and I've come back to the area with my family to live and work.

It's no secret that my time with the club came to a bit of a sour end, and that was largely down to Tony Petty and the eventual new board.

I remember the day I was fired. Basically, Tony Petty just called us into the office one by one and said, 'You're sacked.' You walk out in a bit of a daze and say, 'He just sacked me. What do we do now then?'

Nick Cusack actually did very well then, as he was our PFA rep and got the PFA involved straight away.

In December 2001 I went to Oxford United on loan, which was initially to help the club out. They [Swansea] couldn't afford the wage bill. Petty had gone by this point and a new board had come in.

I really didn't enjoy being at Oxford and I actually asked to come back to Swansea, but I was told I wasn't allowed to come back, and that I should find somewhere else. That's something the Swans fans never knew.

Incredibly, the new board at Swansea wouldn't actually communicate with me. In fact, they would only speak to me through Don Goss, who was the stadium safety officer at the time. He was my only point of contact, which was disgraceful.

So, a decision was made by myself and my agent to find another club, and Oxford turned the loan deal into a permanent contract.

The Swans fans didn't like this at all. They thought I had done it for myself, and they were calling me a greedy bastard and so on.

But what they don't know is that I had an 18-month contract left with the Swans, and that I had taken a 40 per cent pay cut to go to Oxford just to get off the Swansea wage bill and help the club out. Huw Jenkins and his lot had conveniently failed to report this to anybody, including the fans.

I ended up making a deal with the new Swans board, where they would pay me a lump sum over the three months, which was a small percentage of what I was owed.

I had the first month's payment, and then they didn't pay me the second month. So, when the club went for a Company Voluntary Arrangement, I voted against clearing all the debts, because that would have been all my money gone.

I felt as though Huw Jenkins had tucked me up, knowing what they were planning – the CVA – when they agreed to the payments over three months. They *did* report to the fans that I had voted against the CVA, although my vote was aimed solely at the new board and not the club.

One of the most upsetting incidents that occurred as a result of this was when I came back to Swansea one weekend with my wife, and one fan spat in her face, which was bang out of order. At that point my blood was boiling and I was ready to go and batter the board, as they had basically made our life a living hell.

When I've spoken to fans, certainly the ones I am still friendly with, they know the real story and the truth over what happened. They understand it.

But I don't hold a grudge – life's too short. If I saw Huw now I would shake his hand. Those were just the circumstances at the time. We're living back in Swansea now and we love it here.

After Oxford I went down to Weymouth for a couple of years, which was great as it was a part-time contract, which allowed me to get back to college and complete some qualifications ahead of my next life.

I was actually taking my financial advisor exams when an opportunity in the tourism industry in Swansea came along. That was a slight change on the career path that I had planned and a big learning curve!

So, I hung up my boots and moved back down to Swansea. The plan always was to move back down here anyway. I absolutely love the area, it's just superb.

I now run HomefromHome, a self-catering holiday cottage business for Swansea, Mumbles and Gower. To be in the holiday and tourism industry really helps us promote the area, and it feels good to give something back.

I've lived in some grotty places in my time, so to come back to Swansea and live in Mumbles – which is so friendly and safe – is just a dream come true for me.

JAMES THOMAS: BORN 16 JANUARY 1979, SWANSEA; 57 GAMES, 16 GOALS

James Thomas

Swansea City 4-2 Hull City
Football League Third Division
The Vetch, 3 May 2003

When it comes to stories of local heroes stepping up to save their football clubs, it's hard to beat the tale of James Thomas. Born in Swansea in January 1979, the striker signed for Blackburn Rovers as a teenager, although he spent the majority of his time loaned out to other clubs. In September 2002 he seized the opportunity to join his home town club on a free transfer and played a critical role in keeping the Swans in the Football League that season, with 15 important goals. The striker was with Swansea for three seasons and played 57 games for the club before injuries played their part in his eventual departure from the game. There's never been any question over which of those 57 was his most memorable.

Swansea City: Cutler, Jenkins, O'Leary, Tate, Howard, Coates, Britton, Martinez, Johnrose, Nugent, Thomas

Hull City: Fettis, Otsemobor, Whittle, Joseph, Smith, Delaney, Melton, Keates, Reeves, Elliott, Burgess

Swansea Scorers: Thomas (3), Johnrose

Hull Scorers: Elliott, Reeves

Referee: S. Mathieson

Attendance: 9,585

WHEN I was asked to contribute my story to this book, there were no prizes for guessing the game I'd choose.

The match against Hull City in May 2003 is remembered as one of the most important games in the history of Swansea City – we know it now, and we knew it at the time.

Being relegated from the Football League would have been disastrous. It's one thing dropping out of the Premier League into the Championship, but to fall out of the Football League into the Conference was the footballing equivalent of hell.

It's so competitive down there. Any team can beat any team and getting back into the league would have been so difficult.

At the time, the Liberty Stadium plans were in place, but everything was on hold to see if we were going to stay up or not. If we'd have gone down, maybe that wouldn't have been built.

From a personal point of view, being from Swansea, survival meant so much to me. My friends and family were all Swans fans, and I felt that everyone was relying on me.

A lot of people at the Vetch that day were friends, family and people from school. I knew a lot of them, whereas some of the other players didn't have that – Swansea was just another football club to them.

I had also followed the Swans since I was younger. I'd have been around 13 or 14 when I first went down there, in the era of John Cornforth, Des Lyttle, and Roger Freestone.

So, it was nice to grow up and go on to play for the club.

I had spent seven years at Blackburn. I joined them in 1996, the season after they won the Premier League. They were the best team in the country then, with players like Chris Sutton and Alan Shearer.

While I was there, I was sent out on loan to West Brom, Blackpool, Sheffield United and Bristol Rovers. I was dotted around left, right and centre. When my contract ran out, I really wanted to start playing first-team football, so when the chance came to join Swansea I found it too hard to turn down.

It was a big thing for me to come back and play for Swansea. There was a lot of personal pride, as not a lot of people get the opportunity to play for their home town club.

It was also a privilege to play with some of the players I had idolised growing up. Like Roger – I had watched him on the pitch when I was a teenager, then suddenly I was playing alongside him, rooming with him, playing *Football Manager* and hanging out with him. That was great.

I came back to Swansea in September 2002, and at that stage the club and fans were full of optimism. We had made a few signings in the summer, and everyone was going into the season fairly positive.

But from pretty early on in the season, it was evident that we would struggle.

I remember – or rather, I keep getting reminded – about the game against Boston United in September, when we hit the very bottom of the Football League. Then it was panic stations – reality hit home.

Personally, I wasn't doing badly and I hit the ground running when it came to scoring. I scored nine goals in 11 games and I felt like I was doing all right. But confidence was low throughout the team and that is always hard to get back.

It's difficult to pinpoint why we had done so badly. A lot of players had come in over the summer and it was hard to get these players to gel together straight away. When that didn't happen and we got off to a bad start, it was hard to gain momentum.

Because resources were limited at Swansea, the calibre of player the club went for was also limited.

Before I joined, I remember coming down for a trial game consisting of about 20 players that had been released from other clubs. The cast-offs from other clubs – that's the reality of it. Looking back now, it's not surprising that we had such a disappointing season.

However, Brian Flynn came in to replace Nick Cusack as manager around ten games in.

I had a bit of a difficult time after he came in, as he changed the formation and started playing me out on the left wing, which wasn't my position. It just didn't suit me, and to this day I can't understand why he did it.

I can't remember how many games I had gone without scoring, but it seemed like everyone was on my back reminding me of this fact.

But playing out on the left side, chances are much more limited compared to when I was playing up top.

I was picking up the paper and that's all I read about – how many games it had been since I last scored. I think I went 18 games in total.

Thankfully, in the last half-dozen or so games, we started picking up some decent results and I started scoring again.

Everyone puts our survival down to the Hull game, and inevitably it was that match that kept us up. But it was the last six or eight games that really changed things.

Make no mistake about it, the penultimate match of the season against Rochdale was a huge game. It was Marc Richards who scored and we won 1-0, which meant survival was in our hands.

We just needed to beat Hull City on the final day of the season.

As a player, it's a huge advantage going into such a big game knowing that you're in control. That's what Exeter didn't have – they had to win *and* rely on us to not win. So, it was advantage us.

The build-up in the week was much bigger than usual and the atmosphere was growing by the day. You could tell something big was happening. After the Rochdale match in particular, the press was all over us. Everyone wanted to speak to you.

This led to an embarrassing moment for me.

Every Friday in training we'd have a little five-a-side match and whoever got voted the worst player that day would have to wear the yellow jersey in the training session the week after.

The week before the Hull game, I had been voted the worst player! So, the day before the Hull game I had the yellow jersey on. It *had* to be the time that twice as many people as normal turned up to our training sessions at Ashleigh Road, and the cameras were there. I was there thinking, 'Well this is a good start, isn't it?'

Being a local boy, perhaps I felt the pressure a bit more than the others. I still had my friends and family reminding me how important it was and telling me not to lose the match. It was all said tongue-in-cheek and they tried to make a joke out of it, but I knew they were serious.

The night before the Hull match I tried to keep calm, but my nerves were terrible. I had run through everything in my head, going through all the ifs and buts.

On the day, the nerves are still there when you get up, but when you arrive at the ground, you focus and your head is on the match, and then it feels like any other game really.

It wasn't until we did the warm-up when it really sunk in.

Alan Curtis pulled all the boys together in a huddle and laid it on the line.

Curt was the type of character who wouldn't say a lot, but when he *did* say something, everyone listened. He's a lovely bloke, he'd never raise his voice, and would put an arm around you when you needed it. A great guy.

That day, in that huddle, his emotions all spilled out as he told us what the club meant to him. If anyone there was unaware of the importance of the game before Curt said what he did, then suddenly they were in no doubt. That helped everyone focus a bit more.

Brian Flynn wasn't a shouter either, and he never waffled on and on. I don't think he even said that much to us before the match, maybe to keep the pressure to a minimum. It was a case of everyone knew what they had to do, so we just went out and did it.

It must have been the 20th game I had played at the Vetch that season, but you couldn't compare it to any other.

The stands were full, the crowd was electric, and the place was rocking. The weather was horrible, but no one cared – everyone had come out to support us.

That day the crowd were definitely the 12th man for us.

We actually had the best possible start to the match as we had a penalty given in the eighth minute. I think even before then I had a few good chances to put us ahead. I hit the post at one stage after Coatesy crossed one in, and another one where I tried to lob the keeper but it went over the bar.

So we started quite well, which was necessary to get the crowd on our side. And they had something to cheer as Britts made that little darting run down the right and was taken down in the box for a stonewall penalty.

While I hadn't been in the best form in the middle of the season, I was scoring goals again as I was playing back up front.

I was the penalty taker and I hadn't missed one, so I was fairly confident, especially as I had scored a penalty a few games before against Southend.

I knew which way I was going. I just shut off from everything around me and hit it into the corner, with the keeper diving the wrong way. Great, we were 1-0 up.

But the crowd barely had time to celebrate because Hull equalised a minute later to get straight back into it; 1-1.

Jenks made the mistake. He's a lovely bloke, but he's a confidence player and if there was anyone you didn't want it to happen to, it was him.

Honestly, he was almost crying on the pitch after that. I remember he told me afterwards that he was taking a throw-in and his hands were shaking so much he could barely throw the ball, especially as the abuse was being hurled at him.

Shortly after, Michael Howard made another mistake and that was Hull's second chance – and they took it. Suddenly, we were 2-1 down.

It was almost like we had blinked and were staring at relegation again. You could hear the animosity in the crowd and the boos started coming out. It was like a cauldron in there.

As the captain, Roberto was a good motivator and he was trying to rally the troops. But a few heads were dropping. It was a very dark time.

But we plugged on and pulled ourselves together, finding our chance to equalise through another penalty just before half-time. It was never a penalty, but we didn't complain!

I had run through the right channel, went to flick the ball over Justin Whittle but it hit him in the chest – he never touched it with his hand. But it was one of those where I stuck my hand up and called for a pen. The ref had the pressure of the home crowd shouting at him and took the easy option as he pointed to the spot.

Taking that second penalty was a completely different kettle of fish.

Nerves were very high, because the atmosphere by that point had completely changed to when I had taken the first one. Whereas the crowd were all positive and cheering before the first penalty, there was more of a dull and moody atmosphere before the second, because we were behind.

It was just before half-time, so the second penalty was far more significant than the first one, and this was all going around in my mind.

But I was never in doubt over whether or not I would take it. I was always going to take it, no matter what.

When I stepped up, I knew which corner I was going to go for, but this time it wasn't a good penalty. Then again, I say it wasn't a good penalty, but I suppose as long as it goes in it *is* a good penalty.

It was more or less straight down the middle. Thankfully the keeper dived. Alan Fettis was in goal for them that day and I used to play with him at Blackburn, so perhaps he dived out of the way to help me!

Because of the timing of it, and the fact that we had been 2-1 down, without a shadow of a doubt that was the most important goal I scored that day. A huge turning point in the game.

It meant we came out for the second half feeling positive, but we knew we still needed another goal – and that actually came a few minutes into the half.

I think it was a corner that had come over and I headed it back towards the goal for Lenny Johnrose to put in. At the time I didn't know who had scored because I was down on the floor injured. I knew we had scored because I could hear the crowd go mad, but I didn't actually see the goal until I watched the highlights.

So, we were 3-2 up, and from that point on Hull didn't want to know.

They were on their holidays and playing for nothing – it was the last game of the season, they were middle of the table, the game meant nothing to them.

As players we've all been there. Mentally you just can't wait to get on the beach after a long season. At that point they just wanted to get up the M4 back to Hull.

The stands were bouncing, we were confident again and, to be honest, from then on there was never any doubt in the result.

But we weren't done.

With 57 minutes on the clock I finished my hat-trick. Coatesy put in a good tackle around the centre circle and the ball broke perfectly in front of me. I didn't have to break stride, I just took a touch past the defender, and then I made the decision.

Actually, no – I didn't have time to make a decision. The first thing that came to my mind was, 'The keeper is off his line – lob him.'

That's what confidence can do for you. You don't dwell on things for too long, you just do the first thing that feels right. I went for the lob and, as it goes, it went in the top corner. It couldn't have worked out any better.

Because we were 3-2 up, I had already scored two, and the atmosphere was so positive, it gave me that opportunity to just go with it.

Seeing the ball sail over Fettis's head and hit the back of the net was just relief.

The weight of the weeks building up to the match was released. Every game had been like a pressure cooker, building up to this point. All that stress and weight was lifted in that moment. I had never felt anything like that before and I probably never will again.

We thought the game had been over at 3-2, but after that final one went in and we were leading 4-2, it had literally become like an exhibition match. You just wanted the ref to blow his whistle.

I remember when the final whistle eventually went, everyone's instinct was to get off the pitch as you could see the wave of supporters engulfing the field.

We all got into the dressing room and I suddenly realised I had forgotten the match ball. Because I had scored a hat-trick, the match ball was officially mine.

Luckily for me, Kev Nugent was about to take a corner as the final whistle went and – fair play to him – he thought of me, grabbed the ball, and ran with it through the crowd. So, when we were in the dressing room he presented it to me, which was brilliant.

All the boys signed it, and I've still got it in the house – it takes pride of place.

Normally after a game like that, I would have kept my shirt too. But that was ripped off me by fans in all the chaos – and my shorts were gone as well. So, as far as my kit went, I had none of that as a keepsake.

It was early on in the next season that a fan actually came up to me with my shirt from that game and asked me to sign it. Not only did he rob my bloody shirt but he wanted me to sign it too!

We had a laugh about it and I signed it for him. I'm just happy I had the ball.

These bits of memorabilia are unique as the Swans will probably never have a game of such importance again. Staying in the Premier League is important, but not really as crucial as it was staying in the Football League.

It was a bit odd as everybody was celebrating like we had just won the league, but in reality, we had only just stayed up from falling out of it completely. That was the lowest of the low.

At the time, I can see why we celebrated, but I was also thinking, 'Right, let's make sure this never happens again.'

As I've said, it was also a feeling of relief as much as it was joy. With me being a local boy, had we been relegated, it would have been a case of me never wanting to show my face in Swansea again, for fear of being lynched by someone. Now, instead, I won't show my face in Cardiff as I was the one that kept the Swans up. That way round, I don't mind so much!

In the dressing room after the match we arranged to meet up in the evening to celebrate. 'We'll all meet in the Pitcher and Piano at eight o'clock – but keep it quiet,' we said.

As planned, we rolled up at the Pitcher and Piano at eight o'clock, and you couldn't see in there for people. It was absolutely rammed.

I don't know how they knew we were meeting there, but someone had let slip and word quickly spread. Next thing you know, there were hundreds of people in there. It was unbelievable. You couldn't move.

We all walked in and suddenly the crowd split down the middle, like parting the Red Sea. Everyone was singing the Swansea songs, throwing themselves at us, handing us drinks. It was one of the best nights I've ever had.

It was so overwhelming, and I think at that stage what we'd achieved properly hit us.

I think I was actually home by about 10.30 that night. Throw in the build-up, the pressures, the game, and the amount of people that evening – I was shattered.

But the night, as well as the day, was just unforgettable.

Sadly, it all went downhill for me the season after that game. I had signed a new two-year contract and we started the season quite well. We won the first game, and the second one against Cheltenham, in which I scored. Things were going really well.

But then, all of a sudden, I was benched and out of the team. I don't know why.

Then I was sort of in and out, playing the last ten minutes here, last ten there. I went from hero of one season to pretty much forgotten in the next.

Injuries crept up and I just couldn't get a run of being in the team or a run of being fit. So, the 2003/04 season was a major disappointment, especially considering how the previous season had ended on such a high.

The season after that, when Kenny Jackett came in, I suffered my knee injury which effectively ended my career.

I saw my two years out with the Swans but by the end of it I was so frustrated for so many reasons. I had become disillusioned with the game. In the end I was almost happy to step back from it all.

After that season finished, I went up to Llanelli after a self-funded knee operation. I thought it was right after that, but it wasn't.

It's hard to describe the frustration of not being able to do something fully because of an injury – I wasn't able to sprint properly because of the pain. In the end, I just said, 'I've had enough,' and called it a day with Llanelli, and hung up my boots.

Despite what it says on the internet, I didn't go to Australia to play after that. I don't know where that story came from. A lot of people ask me about that, but I've never even been to Australia for a holiday, let alone to play for a football team there. It's bizarre.

What is true is that I am now an ambulance driver. When I finished playing football, finding a career was difficult because, from the day I left school at 16 years old, all I had known was football. Once that had been taken away from me unexpectedly, I felt a bit stuck.

I'll always remember about a year after I left the Swans, myself and my wife bumped into Roberto and his wife in town. So, we went for some food together and he said to me, 'Do your coaching badges now and there'll be a job down here for you for life.'

At the time, I was still disillusioned with the game, and didn't want anything to do with it. I was still peed off with the injury and the frustration, and I basically said, 'Thanks for the offer, but no thanks.'

Not taking him up on that offer is probably one of my biggest regrets really.

It wasn't until a year or two after that that I began to think, 'I'm missing day-to-day football.' The playing, the banter, the lifestyle. But it was too late. I had started a new career, and felt I had been out of the game for too long to be able to get back in.

My sister's husband was a paramedic, and he told me to try for a job in the ambulance service. The job was non-emergency patient transport to start with. I did my exams, passed the driving test, and got through the interview – that was actually my first ever interview!

That was back in 2008. Now, ten years later, I'm on the front line, working as an emergency medical technician [EMT], which means I go out to all sorts of emergency situations.

Don't get me wrong, I'd still rather be doing something with football, but it's a good job and still gets the adrenalin going like it used to when I was playing football. It's nice to be out and about, not stuck in an office like I could have done. I'm lucky to have it.

I still follow the Swans and had a season ticket for the first four years of the Premier League. But since moving into the emergency side of my job, I'm working a lot of weekends, so don't go down as much anymore.

It goes without saying that I would have loved to have been part of the club a few years later, and to have played at the Liberty Stadium. Lovely fans, lovely stadium, lovely pitch – it certainly makes me a bit jealous.

Don't get me wrong, you can't beat the Vetch and the old North Bank for atmosphere. But put those facilities and the pitch next to what they have now and it just doesn't compare.

However, it was nice to have played in Alan Tate's testimonial, to get my boots on and experience playing there because I had never had the opportunity until that point.

I never really thought about that day against Hull much after the game itself – until we got to the Premier League. Of course, I knew the importance of it at the time, but in the years that followed there was a big gap of it never being mentioned.

It wasn't until Swansea hit the Premier League that it became relevant again.

In fact, my phone didn't stop ringing. To go from where we had been to the biggest league in the world in such a short space of time, suddenly everyone wanted to talk about it.

That's when you start thinking, 'Where would the club have been after that day if we had gone down?' So many people were talking about it, and it reminds you that, yes – it was that important.

Because the Hull game was where it all started.

LEE TRUNDLE: BORN 10 OCTOBER 1976, LIVERPOOL; 166 GAMES, 82 GOALS

Lee Trundle

Swansea City 2-1 Carlisle United

Football League Trophy Final

Millennium Stadium, 2 April 2006

In August 2003, just months after Swansea City escaped relegation from the Football League, Lee Trundle arrived to inject life into a club desperately in need of some positivity. Armed with a lethal finish, an arsenal of tricks and genuine club pride, Trundle became an instant fan favourite, with his popularity growing every year. 'Magic Daps' went on to spend four seasons with the club, scoring 77 league goals in his first stint, then a further five when he returned to play for the Swans on loan in 2009. Trundle still plays football part-time, while he remains an important presence at Swansea, having held the position of club ambassador since 2013.

Swansea City: Gueret, Ricketts, Monk, Lowe, Tate, O'Leary (Knight), Britton, Robinson (Martinez), Tudur-Jones, Akinfenwa, Trundle

Carlisle United: Westwood, Livesey, Gray, Arnison (Grand), Aranalde, Murphy, Billy, Lumsdon, A. Murray (Hackney), Holmes (Murray), Hawley

Swansea Scorers: Trundle, Akinfenwa

Carlisle Scorer: A. Murray

Referee: A. Leake

Attendance: 42,028

AS STRANGE as it may sound, the fact that we were about to play in a cup final finally hit me the moment we were all dressed in our suits.

Watching the FA Cup on the telly as a kid, you always used to see the players turning up to cup finals in their special suits. So, for me, wearing our own suits was a very big thing.

Our suits that day were real rascal suits – black and white pinstripe, with a big bright pink tie. It was a bit loud to say the least!

Going into the ground all dressed up really brought it home that it was a cup final, and that was just a dream come true for me.

At the time it was genuinely like getting to the FA Cup Final for Swansea. Where we were in the league and where we were as a football club, to get to a final at the Millennium Stadium was just brilliant.

As far as I was concerned, I *was* going to play in the FA Cup Final.

I don't think anyone was surprised that we had made it that far though. We had been very confident that season and, from the moment the cup ties were drawn, we believed we could go all the way.

We were doing well in the league, challenging for promotion, and I think that confidence pours over into cup runs.

When you're winning games, you get into that mentality where your confidence is high and you go out believing that you're going to win every match.

That doesn't mean we went in *expecting* to win the final though. Everyone knows the deal with cup matches – anything can happen.

As a team, you're always confident of success if you're in the league above your opposition, but there honestly isn't that much difference between League 1 and League 2.

Carlisle were a solid team, with a good goalscorer in Karl Hawley, who was always a threat. They had beaten some good teams to progress in the cup and were in the final for a reason, so we never took them lightly.

I can't remember much about our road to the final because, for a lot of those games, I would have been a sub. The Football League Trophy was a competition where we would rotate players, with those not playing in the league given a chance in the cup.

Up top at the time, we had me, Bayo, Rory Fallon and Leon Knight. At that level you had four very good forwards who were all good goalscorers.

We played a direct 4-4-2 and, in the league, it would mostly be me and Bayo up front, with Leon and Rory coming on as subs, as well as starting most of the cup games.

It was only as we got to the quarters and semis that we began putting out our strongest side, and I would have started those games.

Given the chance though, I would have played every single match. I'm the type of player who always wants to be out on the pitch. I just love playing football. But I also knew that promotion in the league was our main aim that season. We wanted to try to get out of League 1, so even though I wanted to play every game, I understood that I was getting rested for the bigger league games coming up.

As Cardiff is so close to Swansea, we travelled down the M4 on the day of the final, instead of staying up there the night before. That was probably great for our fans too, as they didn't have far to travel either.

The Swans fans made the most of it because, as we drove in on the coach, you could see the streets of Cardiff had been turned into Swansea.

Black and white scarfs, Jack Army flags and Swans shirts were everywhere. Our fans were banging on the side of the coach and waving to us – seeing all that gave me a massive buzz. I couldn't wait to get going.

But it was excitement, not nerves. I was never nervous in games, I just loved being out there. The bigger the game, the more I enjoyed it.

Growing up as a kid, you dream of playing in these cup finals. I just couldn't wait to get out there, to play in front of a huge crowd, including about 20 of my family and friends who had travelled down from Liverpool for the game.

Forty-two thousand is a lot of people to play in front of, plus the game was on Sky so you had millions of people watching from their homes across the country.

That would have been the biggest crowd I had ever played in front of. You work all your life in football to get in front of those big crowds and, while I wasn't nervous, I remember I felt a little bit light-headed in the dressing room before the game, almost as if I was walking on air.

It was the first time I had ever been to the Millennium Stadium and it was unbelievable.

To have so many people in such a massive, imposing stadium was brilliant. The roof was closed that day, which kept the noise in and made the atmosphere even stronger.

Of course, it was our fans you could hear the most, probably because we outnumbered Carlisle supporters by quite a few thousand!

Surprisingly, for such an impressive stadium, the pitch that day wasn't the best. I'm not sure what events they'd had on beforehand, but it actually wasn't as good as what we were used to down the Liberty. It was patchy and a bit slippery on the top.

Still, it didn't matter too much, especially as we had the dream start. After just three minutes, I put us ahead with the best goal I ever scored for Swansea.

Carlisle had the ball and their keeper was playing it out when I charged it down. He went to clear it, but it hit my side and broke to one of their players. Andy Robinson got a tackle in and put the ball to Leon, who was on the far right of the pitch. He lofted the ball over to me on the far side.

The ball was in the air for a long time, and I just thought, 'Get your shot off early, and let the keeper know you're going to be doing this all game.'

It fell to my chest and, instead of letting it drop, I hit it on the volley and it flew into the far corner.

The technique of the shot was brilliant, as I put it in the only place the keeper wouldn't have been able to reach it.

It's nice to think of doing something and then watch it come off perfectly – because I've had plenty of shots where I've been thinking one thing, then done something completely different!

So, to hit a shot like that, mean it, and see it come off, was even more special.

When you watch the video of the game back, it looks like I'm really aggressive as I run over to the crowd just after I've scored my goal – I almost look angry because I'm shouting.

But it wasn't aggression, it was just the pent-up energy and emotion from the build-up that came pouring out.

In the warm-up, I had spotted where my family and friends were sitting in the top tier, so I ran over to them to celebrate.

To score a goal like that in a cup final, with all your family and friends watching, was just a great release and a brilliant feeling, and that's all it was.

I'll always remember – and you can see on the video – Tatey grabbed me as the celebrations died down and shouted, 'You're the man, you're the man!'

One goal up after a few minutes, we continued to push forward to get another.

Andy Robinson had a great chance where he could have scored, and we also had a few other half-chances after that in the first half – but so did Carlisle.

At one stage, around 20 minutes in, Karl Hawley put the ball in the net for Carlisle, but that goal was disallowed for offside. That was a reminder that they were more than capable of getting back on level terms, which is exactly what they did just before half-time.

They had a throw-in in our half, it was flicked on, then Adam Murray headed it past Willy. That was a bit of a blow, but even then, I always believed we had enough and would go on to win the game.

Plus, while there's never a great time for the opposition to score, it's better for them to score just before half-time.

If they had have scored early in the second half, they would have had the momentum to keep them going. But scoring five minutes before the ref blows for the half gives us 15 minutes to regroup.

As we got into the changing room at half-time, it was a case of 'more of the same' from the manager. We were the better side, we'd had most of the play and most of the chances in the first half.

We knew we had to keep it a bit tighter at the back, because they were dangerous and if they got a half-chance they could turn it into a goal.

Kenny Jackett just told us to believe in ourselves because we were the best team out there.

From what I can remember, the second half was pretty tight and it wasn't as exciting as the first. We had a couple of chances, and Robbo and Bayo had at least one decent shot each, but Carlisle had a few chances from set pieces too. I don't think I had anything on target in the second half.

I can't remember who was marking me that day, but then again, I was one of those players that never took notice of the opposition.

Some players will study other players, watching them to see what they do. But I think the more you look at someone like that, you set a bit of doubt in your own game, especially if they are particularly good at something.

I would prefer to go out with a blank mind and play my own game. I believed that if I did that, I would always get the better of any defender I came up against.

To me though, confidence is the secret to being a good striker.

When a striker is scoring goals, they are always confident and believe in themselves. It's when they go a few games without a goal that a vicious circle can begin.

Look at Fernando Torres with Liverpool – every half-chance he got, he was sticking it away. He goes to Chelsea and, although they play a different way and he didn't have the same support, it takes him 23 games to score a goal. His confidence just kept going down and down.

If you haven't got confidence as a striker, you become a completely different player. You start thinking about every touch, every shot.

But you look at me in that final – as soon as that ball is coming over, I'm not worried about where the ball is going to go. I was high on confidence and it goes in.

Whereas, if I hadn't scored for 15 games, I probably wouldn't have tried to do that. I'd have tried to take a touch, been safer, and probably wouldn't have scored.

Anyway, it was late on in the game when the occasion finally started to catch up with me.

The fatigue began creeping in, after all the adrenalin in the build-up and the highs of scoring the goal. It was around 75 minutes in and I felt a bit tired, and started thinking, 'I really hope this doesn't go to extra time.'

But then a few minutes later we ensured it wouldn't.

The ball came to me, I turned someone and then put it through to Bayo. He's run on and used his strength – the great physical presence that he is – to finish it. I think the keeper had a touch, but it looped up and into the goal. What a feeling as soon as that goal went in.

We were ahead with less than ten minutes left. It didn't stop Carlisle trying for another equaliser and they threw everything at us. They had a chance late on, which Willy tipped over the bar. That was a great save.

We tried to go down the other end and keep the ball. I remember doing a little bit of showboating in the corner to waste some time.

It was a classic one – I would pretend to pick up the ball, but then kick it away with my foot. I think the ref saw it as taking the micky, so he told me to stop it or he would book me!

I wasn't trying to disrespect the opposition, that was just me enjoying the cup final.

I had done a bit of showboating through the game – as everyone knows, that was the kind of player I was and how I enjoyed playing football.

On an occasion like that, there was a carnival atmosphere with the fans, and that was my way of giving them some extra entertainment. Any time I could get the crowd involved, that's what I would do, whether it was doing a trick or giving them a wave.

If I'm going to watch a match, I like to be entertained. I think football fans like to go to a match to see players do things they can't do themselves. We can all pass a ball, but not everyone can do a trick.

I have certain tricks I'll perform in certain areas of the pitch, where I know they'll work for me to gain some space to get away. Most of my tricks would be in the opposition's 18-yard box, definitely not in my own half.

There were tricks that would be effective in creating a chance and helping me get a shot off, and there were other ones where you'd antagonise players to entice them into making a tackle on you. That way you could draw a foul and kill the game a bit. If I was wasting time to see a game out, maybe I would do one of those in the corner.

When you're doing that in the corner, that's what I would call showboating. The other tricks are a type of skill, as I'm usually trying to go past a man to get a shot off, or get a cross in, or create a chance for a team-mate.

I wouldn't just be doing them for the sake of it – there was always an end product.

I would also make sure I could pull the trick off. Every single day I would practice, practice, practice until I had nailed it.

I would do them in the practice matches we had in training, then I would stay behind after training and practice little moves by myself, going around cones then hitting it into an empty net.

As well as making up my own tricks, I loved watching players like Gazza and Ronaldo – the Brazilian one – as they had brilliant skills.

Funnily enough, a lot of my most successful tricks started as another trick that went wrong. But even though the trick didn't come off, I would think, 'Hang on, I could use that as a different trick.'

One of the tricks I use all the time – which is now known as 'The Trundle' – was the result of another one going wrong, but it works better than I could have imagined, and now it's my favourite as it sends the defender in the complete opposite direction to me.

It's been said I used to send clips of myself doing tricks into the show *Soccer AM*, but that's not entirely true.

The kind of show that it was, they loved the showboating and wanted to get the clips on. But they would have to watch a full game to find the tricks so they could make a montage of them.

In the end, to save them time, they would text me at the end of the game to ask me to give them the rough times that I had done the tricks, so they could find them quicker. So, I never sent anything in, but I would send them the rough times of the tricks to help out.

Going back to the final, we successfully held Carlisle off for the remaining ten minutes – and I didn't get a booking in the end!

It was unbelievable as the match ended, especially when we had the trophy celebration on the pitch, with the flames shooting up behind us and the crowd roaring. It was a great feeling.

Garry Monk was captain that day, but he made sure Roberto was there to lift the trophy with him too, which was a nice touch.

Then came an incident that eventually ended up with me being arrested.

As we were walking around, celebrating with the Swans fans, I ended up holding that infamous flag – as well as putting on an offensive t-shirt that showed a character wearing a Swans shirt peeing on a Cardiff shirt.

The thing is, there were so many flags and t-shirts being thrown on from the crowd at the end, I genuinely wasn't aware of what I was holding up. Because we also had some official white t-shirts with 'Cup Final Winners' on the front, I thought I was picking up one of those.

Even so, at the end of the day, the t-shirts we were wearing were the kind of thing you'd see on car bumper stickers. It's a bit of tongue-in-cheek humour.

Personally, I don't find that kind of thing offensive in football, as you see it everywhere – Liverpool v Everton, Man City v Man United, and Swansea v Cardiff. They're massive rivals, so you can expect that kind of thing.

But the t-shirts, combined with the flag, definitely caused a stir. Both me and Tatey were arrested for it, we got an ASBO for four years, a one-match ban, and I was fined one week's wages.

I think any Swansea fan – having just won a cup in their rival's city – would have loved to have done the same out on the pitch. Looking at me on the pitch with the flag and t-shirt, they probably saw a bit of themselves.

For that, it's something that Swans fans still speak to me about to this day.

The sad thing was, all of the papers the next day were more concerned about the t-shirt and banning me, than us winning the cup and the goal I scored. No one talked about the match, and that was a shame.

One thing I also remember from that day was that we carried round a little handheld video camera to record the occasion. We made a video diary of the day before the game, where some of the lads were in town asking fans who was going to win, who was going to score, and things like that.

Then we filmed on the coach on the way up to the game, as well as getting some footage of us on the pitch celebrating the win.

We also had footage of us all having a good sing-song on the coach on the way home. Rory Fallon used to play the guitar, so he brought his along for that trip and played while we sang, which was great.

The club mixed our video together with footage from the game and player interviews, and put it all into a DVD, then sold it in the club shop. I think it's called *The Millennium Final*, or something like that. I'm not sure if you can still find it, but it's a good watch, and brings back great memories of that time.

When we got back to Swansea, we went to Morgan's Hotel to celebrate as a team with our friends and families. I think there was a free bar too, so there was champagne all over the place. It was a brilliant way to celebrate a great day.

Sadly, our next trip to the Millennium Stadium – just a month later for the League 1 play-offs – didn't end in celebrations.

Because we had won there against Carlisle, we believed we would win again against Barnsley on 27 May.

I was on the bench that day, although it was a game that I felt I should have been playing.

But Leon Knight did really well in the semi-final against Brentford and scored a hat-trick, so Kenny dropped me and went with Rory and Leon for the final.

They are the type of games I thrive in, and I should have been on from the start. I did come on towards the end and managed to get a shot off, but that went just wide of the post.

I also stepped up to take the first penalty and scored that. But we eventually went out through the shoot-out and that's a terrible way to lose. Still, it was the only way to decide the game.

One thing I made sure to do was stay out on the pitch with Andy Robinson after we lost to watch the Barnsley players lift the trophy.

In a strange way I wanted it to hurt me, so next time I was in that situation I wouldn't have to feel that pain.

I sat there and watched them celebrate. If I'm being honest, I was crying when they were doing it. But it allowed me to use that pain as motivation.

I've just highlighted two very different days of very different emotions taking place within a month. But overall, the time I spent with Swansea was the highlight of my career.

I enjoyed my time on the pitch and my life in Swansea, and that's why I find myself still living here now.

Genuinely, I hope this is the only football club I'm ever involved with. I love my role as club ambassador, it's something that I really enjoy.

I look at people like Curt, who has done so much for the club, and if I can emulate the kind of impact he's had I'll be happy.

It's important to keep people who love and care for the club around it. Curt has been that before, I'm like that now, and the likes of Leon and Angel will have a big future at the club when they finish playing.

While I'm loving my role with Swansea, I also still love playing football.

I'm playing for Llanelli Town at the age of 41, which actually isn't a surprise to me. Even from a young age I didn't see myself hanging up my boots when I reached a certain age. I love football and even at 41, I can't see me stopping any time soon.

Perhaps it might not be at the level I'm playing at now in the Welsh League – I might have to drop down if my legs slow down.

But I also play for an over-40s team on a Sunday, and know of over-45, over-50 and over-55 teams in the area – so I've still got a few years left in me yet!

If I'm honest, I probably work harder now with my training than when I was playing full-time football.

Of course, playing for Swansea I would have always been out on the pitch too, so now I'm not as sharp as I was back then. But the nutrition side of things, and the strength and conditioning aspects weren't really around when I was playing.

I'm getting into that now that I'm older and I think that's a massive part of why I'm still playing. I'll do my own work in the gym, I'll do circuits classes, and I also work with a strength and conditioning coach for injury prevention.

Off the pitch, I'm doing everything right to try to keep myself playing at the highest level I can, for as long as I can.

ALAN TATE: BORN 2 SEPTEMBER 1982, EASINGTON; 293 GAMES, 5 GOALS

Alan Tate

Reading 2-4 Swansea City
Football League Championship Play-Off Final
Wembley Stadium, 30 May 2011

There's a reason Swans fans dream of a team of Alan Tates! Arriving on loan from Manchester United in 2003, Tate firmly cemented himself as a fan favourite for his determination and loyalty to Swansea City. A key part of the 2003 Football League survival campaign, Tate joined Swansea permanently the following season and proved a valuable asset as the Swans climbed the league pyramid. The versatile, tough-tackling defender played his part in the final push into the Premier League, although suffered an injury that halted his career. After over a decade and more than 300 games with the club, Tate left Swansea in 2015. However, after hanging up his boots, he returned to work as a coach for the under-18 squad. If any of the youngsters turn out half as determined as Tate, they'll go very far indeed.

Swansea City: De Vries, Rangel, Williams, Monk, Tate, Allen (Moore), Britton (Gower), Dobbie (Pratley), Dyer, Sinclair, Borini

Reading: Federici, Griffin (Robson-Kanu), Mills, Khizanishvili, Harte, Karacan, Leigertwood, McAnuff, Kebe, Long, Hunt (Church)

Swansea Scorers: Scott Sinclair (3), Stephen Dobbie

Reading Scorers: Joe Allen (og), Matt Mills

Referee: P. Dowd

Attendance: 86,581

A COUPLE of hours earlier, Wembley had been absolutely packed. But as I sat there on the advertising hoarding all by myself, the stadium was silent. It gave me the space to try to take it all in.

'This might not be real,' I was thinking.

Getting into the Premier League. Never in a million years is it something you would imagine happening to you.

After the LDV Final in 2006, I remember I didn't really take everything in properly. So, this time, after we celebrated in the changing room, I grabbed a bottle of beer and went back out into the empty stadium. I sat on the advertising hoardings and just reflected on what had happened.

It was hard to believe, but it wasn't a surprise that we had made it to where we were.

We always had the belief that we could get into the Premier League. We had just missed out on the play-offs the previous season, so there was never any doubt about us being able to do it.

It was always mentioned that we were looking to get promotion no matter how, whether it was winning the league or in the play-offs – and we had done it through the play-offs.

We had made it to Wembley after beating Forest in the semi-finals. Of the two games, the main one that springs to people's minds is beating them 3-1, but for me, the first leg, where we drew 0-0 away from home, was the most important.

Tayls got sent off within two minutes after a high tackle. Monks came on as centre-half, meaning I suddenly had to go from centre-half to left-back.

Even though you're focused, it does cross your mind, 'Ten men; not now. Not in the semi-final. We've done so well to get here, is this going to be taken away from us?'

But at that stage, even though things had been mixed up, we could trust each other as a back four, as we had played together for years. We all just dug in for 90 minutes.

Mentally, I think that's what put us on top going into the second leg. I think coming out of the game, Forest are probably thinking, 'Well, we couldn't beat them with ten men, how can we go and beat them at their place with 11?'

Then we won 3-1 in the second leg at the Liberty, with Leon getting the first one and Pratts getting the killer goal. You can't really describe the emotion of what we were feeling then.

I've heard Gary Neville describe it as an out-of-body experience, when they played against Barcelona in '99, and it was exactly the same for me.

You can't comprehend what's happening. That was the semi-final, but it was exactly the same feeling in the final. People always say to me, 'Going into the game at Wembley, I bet you were buzzing, I bet you had goose bumps listening to Kev Johns.' But no. I can't remember Kev Johns speaking. I can't remember who was behind me in the tunnel. I can't even remember coming out of the tunnel.

I remember we went up to London two days before the game. We trained at Arsenal. We didn't really do anything different to prepare for the game, although we did practise penalties – just in case.

I missed mine. But it's all right because I was never going to take one in the final anyway. I stopped taking penalties after the League 1 play-off in 2006, so it was never really a worry for me.

We also went to have a look around Wembley before we played, but I can't remember if it was before or after the Champions League Final, which was also held there that weekend.

I had been to Wembley before – I went to the United v Chelsea FA Cup Final there in 2007, but I had never been out on the pitch.

I think it was a bigger pitch than the one at the Liberty, but it was lovely and suited the way we played. On the day of the final, after such a sunny morning, it started raining a bit before the match and I think that also helped our game.

We were staying at a nice hotel in London. I was never really one to worry before a game, so I had a good night's sleep.

The weather was boiling in the morning. We were up and downstairs quite early, with our suits on, ready to go. I was sat outside the hotel with Mark Gower, just talking. Nothing about the game, we just sat there chatting, waiting for the other lads to come out.

We then jumped on the bus to Wembley. I can't remember what Brendan said before the match, but it didn't take a manager's speech to get me ready for a game.

I was always ready for it, no matter if it was a play-off final, or a Johnstone's Paint Trophy first-round match, or even a friendly.

I was always ready. That's just how I was.

It sounds odd, but I wasn't more motivated because it was a big game. For me, it was exactly the same as any other game.

Yes, you're aware of how many people are there in the stadium, but they never really played a part in changing my frame of mind. Seeing the Reading fans didn't intimidate me and seeing our own fans didn't boost me. You can hear it, you're aware of it, but I just tried to stay level and not pay attention to it.

Actually, the biggest thing I felt as I came out on to the pitch was the heat coming off those big flames at the side of the tunnel!

We didn't really start the match very well. Reading started on top, without really creating anything. We were never under the cosh, we just didn't have a great start.

I was marking Jimmy Kebe. For some strange reason, which I can never work out, there was a big fuss over him. People were saying, 'Jimmy Kebe – he's brilliant, he's this, he's that,' but it all came from a game in 2008 when they beat us 4-0.

We were playing them away, just after we were promoted from League 1 and they had been relegated from the Premier League.

They brought Kebe in and he played against Fede Bessone. Kebe had a day where everything went right for him. As soon as that happens, your fans think, 'He must do that every week.'

But come the return game here in the league, we beat them 2-0. I played left-back against him and I battered him.

Then, the season after, I played against him as a left-back again and I battered him again. Then the season we got promoted, I played against him twice as a left-back and battered him both times.

So, when everyone was talking about the play-off final, saying 'Jimmy Kebe's going to do this, he's going to do that,' I'm thinking, 'I've played against him five times, and he's never done anything.'

Nothing was going to change, so I knew that, going into the game, the first chance I had to get some contact on him I was going to make a mark.

I knew he wasn't great with the ball, but he was quick. So, I was never going to race him because he was faster than me. But if I could leave one on him I knew he didn't have the heart that I did.

Early in the match we both went up for a ball. I got into the air, won the header, and got my elbow in the back of his head. After that, he didn't want to know.

Yes, he had a good couple of runs, but he was never a great crosser of the ball, and I sort of took that avenue away from him. I knew then that it was game over for him.

You sort of test people. You think, 'If I get a 50-50 with him, and I get the ball and I catch him, will he want to know?' Some attacking players don't. The best ones get up and go again. He didn't and I knew that from the first times I had played against him.

Both teams settled into the game well and about halfway through the first half we got a penalty. I played a good pass into Nath and he was fouled in the area by Zurab Khizanishvili. I think Khizanishvili was lucky really, because he had already been booked. But for whatever reason the ref decided not to give him another yellow card for the foul.

That would have made it easier for us! Scoring a penalty and them down to ten men, that would have made the rest of the game a bit simpler. But we just took any goal in the play-off final as it came.

After Scott had scored, we had the mentality to go and get another. We didn't just want to sit back and protect a 1-0 lead – but we didn't expect to get another just two minutes later. Again, it was Scotty who scored after Dobbs set him up.

Reading had some chances, but we stayed solid at the back. Me, Ash, Monks and Angel. It wasn't your conventional back four, because I'm not really a left-back. But playing there, it just worked. We kept loads of clean sheets that season.

I always preferred to play at centre-half, but when Roberto put me in at left-back ahead of Fede Bessone and Marcos Painter, it just worked. I was quite comfortable at left-back, right-back or even centre-midfield. I even played in goal twice!

As the first half came to an end, Dobbs scored his goal and we went into the break 3-0 up. But I remember as we went into the changing room, it was me, Garry and Ash – we were always the most vocal anyway – who made our voices heard.

'It's only half-time, don't think it's done. Make sure we go and get the next goal.'

The message from Brendan was pretty much the same. 'It's only half-time, it's not over. They've got nothing to lose now. It's only you who can lose it.'

You can say what you want in the changing room, but it doesn't necessarily happen in reality, because when we came out we conceded the next two.

After their first goal we didn't think much of it because we had that two-goal cushion. You're probably thinking, 'Yeah they've got one, but it doesn't matter – we can get back on the ball.' It probably wasn't until they scored their second that, as a team, we fully refocused. I think even then, after the second, it wasn't until Monks' block that it fully clicked.

'Right, you've nearly chucked away this three-goal lead, so get back on it.'

Monks' block was massive. It was an iconic moment in us getting promoted. An iconic moment in the club's history.

I think it was probably the most important block for Swansea as a football club after Neil Cutler's save against Hull in 2003. Because, at the end of the day, if Reading had scored, we were still in the game. If Hull had scored, we were out of the league completely.

Me, Ash and Monks started shouting at a few of the lads, telling them to get themselves going. We made a sub, with Mark Gower coming on at around 60 minutes, then we sort of refocused and became the better team again.

They started the first and second halves as the better team, but we were better in the later stages of both halves.

It's hard to say whether or not they would have gone on to win it had they scored the next goal. With the momentum they had, possibly. But with our team, the characters we had, the resilience we had, and the goals we had, I couldn't see us not scoring again – we always had that goal in us.

It got to the 79th minute and I read the pass from their centre-half. He tried to put it to Kebe's feet, but I got in front of him.

I ran up towards the box, played a through ball to Fabio, and their full-back took him down, which gave us the penalty and our opportunity for the fourth.

As Scott was waiting over the ball I thought, 'Goal.' Never ever doubted him. There were probably only two people who would get a penalty and you'd think, 'Goal,' and that was Jason Scotland and Scott Sinclair. I never ever felt they were going to miss. Never.

Defensively, Scott was a frustrating player at times, but he made up for it with his goals. For me, he was great for the club. That season, he was the single reason we got promoted, in terms of his goals. He was massively important for the club, as was Brendan.

Yes, you had the rest of us, who pitched in and did our bit, but without Scotty's goals we wouldn't have gone as far as we did. And he wouldn't have come to Swansea if it wasn't for Brendan. So, for me, the two go hand in hand.

It was 4-2, it got to the 90th minute, and by then we knew it was won.

You're fully aware of everything in the game, but for those last two minutes, I couldn't begin to tell you what happened – and I've watched the game back three or four times. The final whistle went. It was over. Surreal. Wow.

In that instant, you're trying to think back to where we had come from, meanwhile not really knowing what's going on.

For me, Leon and Garry who had played in the bottom league together, it was brilliant. Ash and Angel were with us in League 1. Darren Pratley was also with us in League 1. It had been a crazy ride. Six lads who had played in the third division together were now suddenly Premier League players together.

To make such a big step in such a short time is crazy really.

Me and Leon were in the Hull game and I think for us to go from one extreme to another is something that no one could have seen happening. It all snowballed from the Hull game, it's unimaginable really.

I don't think it will happen again in such a short space of time. It might if someone pumps a lot of money into a lower league club, but there wasn't really that much money pumped into us.

Swansea was a fan-owned club, the chairman made good decisions along the way with the managers that we got in, and it was something that no one could have predicted.

When Monks lifted the trophy that day, I had actually already gone past him. I thought that Monks was last and was going to pick up the trophy last. So, I'd just walked down the stand, past the trophy, towards Martin Morgan who was giving me a big hug.

I'm there shaking hands with the chairman and, as I look up, Gazza is lifting the trophy! So, I darted back. That's why, if you look at the pictures, it's me first and Monks second, when it should have been the other way around!

I loved the celebrations at the end, when we were spraying each other with champagne. There were the 'We Are Going Up' flags and my medal, which I had around me for ages.

We also had the Besian [Idrizaj, who died aged 22 from a heart attack in 2010 while a Swansea player] t-shirts, which was a nice touch from the club and something that was close to the players, because Bes was our team-mate the year before. Little things like that were brilliant.

After getting the trophy and being out with the fans, we went back into the changing rooms and had a bit of a celebration. Then I went outside to sit on the hoardings.

Sat out there, having a drink, I was quite emotional. You look back and think how far we had come and where we were going.

Not only that, but you think of the life-changing event that it is. Once we were promoted we all had different bonuses and things in our contracts that meant our money would go up, meaning you could look after your family for the rest of your life – if you were sensible.

That's the only promotion that can be life-changing really, and that's what it was to all of us.

I think if we had have had Fabio from the start of the season we would have won the league, but I wouldn't swap winning the league for Wembley. People say the play-off final is the best way to go up and I fully agree with that.

But I've also lost one as well and that's not nice at all. If you can guarantee you're going to get to the play-off final and win it – which you can't – that's the best way to go up.

We came back to Swansea the same night. Every time I have been promoted it seems to be away from home – at Bury, at Gillingham, at Wembley. Because of this, the bus journeys back are always the best.

You've all been together throughout the year, and you're all together on the same bus home. There's no outside influences, there's no camera phones or recordings. It's just you and the lads you've come a long way with.

When we got back to Swansea, the club had put on a party in Morgan's Hotel. But we had the open-top bus parade the next day and I remember waking up with the biggest hangover in the world.

We met down at the hotel where the bus was leaving, and me and Monks just had to get more drink. What makes you bad, makes you better! That was the way we looked at it.

I remember we looked at each other and he said to me, 'Corona?', and I said, 'Yeah, get me a Corona.'

After the summer break, the new Premier League season started and I was in the squad for the first three games. I had started as captain against Man City in the opening match of the season, then I was sub for the Wigan and Sunderland games.

But then, on the Sunday of the August bank holiday, I broke my leg in an accident involving a golf buggy.

I've heard all the stories, but it was just an accident – there was nothing stupid going on. I wasn't drunk, I wasn't sitting on top of it, I was just driving it normally. I lost control of it going downhill on wet grass and we headed straight into a tree.

I had a choice to make – either stay in the cart and possibly hit my head, or jump out. You look at Michael Schumacher now and I think I would take a broken leg over a head injury. Rightly or wrongly, I jumped out and got caught between the buggy and the tree.

Still, I didn't really worry. It's an injury that could have happened in a game, so that's how I approached it.

My attitude was that nothing was too bad, I just got on with it. It was like, 'Right, I've broken my leg, how quickly can I get fit?'

If the doctor tells me six months, I'll prove him wrong and do it in four. If he says it's a year, I'll be back in six months. Even if our physio Kate told me I'd be out for a week, I'd be back in three days.

That was always my mentality. You were injured, but you just got on with it.

With my broken leg, I was out for around four months, but was training with the first team in December, then was back in the squad in January for the FA Cup. I never felt I missed out on anything.

I ended up playing around eight top-flight games with Swansea, but I don't think I was ever going to be a regular Premier League player, where I could play week-in, week-out.

That level was probably a step too far for me. I think I could have played against the bottom five or six teams maybe, but when you start getting up there with the athletes who have a good footballing mind, that's where I would struggle.

I was quite bright as a player and I could read the game well. But having never been the quickest player, when you get up to the Premier League and come up against players who are both athletes *and* intelligent footballers, that's when I couldn't really compete.

As a defender, you are coming up against people who are quicker than you, brighter than you, bigger than you, stronger than you, and that's when you know your level.

I left Swansea in 2015 and wanted to sign for Hartlepool, because I always fancied a couple of years at home.

I had left home when I was 16, so it would have been nice to go back and play up there. I still have friends and family up there who I don't get to see that often. So, I went up to Hartlepool for three weeks, just to get fit and have a look at them.

I sat in with the chief executive on the Thursday and agreed a two-year deal. It wasn't about the money, because it wasn't good money anyway. It was just about getting back home.

They were playing Wimbledon on the Saturday, so I travelled and trained with them on the Friday, then trained with them again on the Monday. But then the manager pulled me in and said it wouldn't be a two-year deal, just the one.

I said, 'Look, I'm not moving my family up here and taking my kids out of school for just one year.'

Once the goalposts had been moved I didn't really trust them, so I just said it wasn't for me. I had been speaking with Port Talbot anyway and because it was close to Swansea, there would be no travelling.

It just made life easier for myself. Train with them once a week, play on a weekend, and get my coaching badges done.

But I did my groin in around February, so I only ended up playing with them for around three months over the winter.

This was a really bad injury, I nearly ripped my groin off. I couldn't move for two weeks. I was coming into Swansea for treatment when I could, and the club were great with me. But I just thought, 'It's not worth it – I don't really want to do it anymore.'

I think it was my body's way of telling me it had done too much. And that was it. I was fully comfortable with my decision. It doesn't bother me not playing, I don't miss it.

I'm currently back with Swansea with the under-18s, along with Anthony Wright and Jon Grey, and I also take the under-18 development team by myself. We all share the responsibilities, but those two take the main under-18s on a Saturday, while I'm responsible for the midweek team.

I love the role. It's sort of me giving back to the club that's given me so much. I want to give these lads a better career than I had. I always tell them you have to aim for the highest level.

You always have to set your goals high. I look back at my career and, ultimately, I failed in what I wanted to do. I wanted to play for Man United for my entire career, but I aimed high and fortunately I still ended up at a good level.

There's not many people that go on to play for Man United for decades, only a couple in history have done that. But growing up as a Sunderland fan, who were never the best team, I thought there's no point in aiming to play for Sunderland for 15 years.

For me, you always try for the best. That's why I ended up going for United, to test myself against the best.

It's well-known that I want to move into management. I think I came out and said it when I sort of knew I was going to pack in playing.

I think what I'm doing now is the best way of learning the job. Believe it or not, even though I played for the club for so long, you never see this side of things. You don't see what happens behind the scenes. This is a good way of learning the trade.

As for the Swans, I go down the Liberty and watch the first team, but I don't wish I was out there. Leon has carried on playing and we are the same age, but body-wise he is better than where I was.

If you look at me, I am not built like an athlete. I was built to take football for so long and that's just how I am.

I got as much out of my career as I could. I wouldn't say I've lived my life as an angel, but I've done as much as I could with what I've got. I've got no regrets about my football career at all.

NATHAN DYER: BORN 29 NOVEMBER 1987, TROWBRIDGE; 260 GAMES, 23 GOALS

Nathan Dyer

Swansea City 5-0 Bradford City
Football League Cup Final
Wembley Stadium, 24 February 2013

After moving around on loan early in his career, Nathan Dyer arrived at Swansea City in 2009 and made the club his home for the next decade. The nippy winger has rarely been far from the team and is always capable of lifting a crowd to their feet as he dances past a defender. He has played in some iconic games for Swansea including the Championship Play-Off Final, the League Cup Final, and a truckload of memorable Premier League and Europa League wins. In 2015, he spent a season on loan with Leicester City – winning the historic Premier League title with the Foxes – before returning to Swansea to continue where he left off.

Swansea City: Tremmel, Rangel, Sung-Yueng (Monk), Williams, Davies (Tiendalli), Britton, de Guzman, Routledge, Dyer (Lamah), Hernandez, Michu

Bradford City: Duke, Darby, Hanson, Thompson (Hines), Atkinson, McHugh, Jones, Wells (McLaughlin), McArdle, Doyle, Good (Davies)

Swansea Scorers: Dyer (2), de Guzman (2), Michu

Referee: K. Friend

Attendance: 82,597

WINNING the League Cup was a great end to our centenary year, but it wasn't a goal we had set out to achieve at the start of the season.

The bigger teams in the league may set out to do that, but smaller teams like Swansea wouldn't necessarily say, 'Right, we're going to put everything in the cup this season and really go for it.'

If you put too much emphasis on it, you don't always get that far, whereas if you take it one game at a time, as we did, then things can start to happen for you.

I don't really remember the four games we played on the road to Wembley. To us, it was just another team and another game, as our main focus was on the league.

It wasn't until we reached the semi-final against Chelsea that we realised we were so close to making history for Swansea.

We had great confidence that season and we were playing great football. Michu was on fire at the time too, which was a big plus, so we went into the Chelsea game looking to show them what we could do.

We were relaxed and able to go and play as we pleased. Michael Laudrup never put any pressure on us and allowed us to express ourselves, which resulted in good performances.

Ultimately, we played Chelsea off the park and walked away with a win in the first leg, then saw out a 0-0 draw at home in the second. Great scenes.

Then came the final at Wembley on 24 February, where we would have the chance to win Swansea's first ever major trophy.

Everyone wanted to go back to Wembley and it was a great opportunity for the boys that hadn't played there with us in the play-offs a few years earlier.

The lead-up to the final was very big with more intense media coverage, especially as we were the favourites playing against Bradford. That was a bit different for us as it's usually the other way around for Swansea going into the big games.

We still prepared as if it was a normal game and Michael didn't overhype the occasion for us, which was good for us as a team.

Looking back, I really enjoyed playing under Michael, because I liked the way he wanted us to play attacking football. He had been a player himself, so he knew how to play that way successfully.

We'd had a bit of a winter break and when we came back we were struggling a bit. Our form wasn't the best and we actually lost 5-0 to Liverpool the week before the final.

But that wasn't a result we carried into the final – a final is a completely different occasion to previous games. A one-off chance, anything can happen.

Our approach towards Bradford was different to how we would have set up if we were taking on a bigger side.

For example, if we were playing someone like Man City, we would have set up more defensively to try to stop them getting through. But for this game we set up to attack Bradford, knowing they would look to ruffle our feathers, kick us around, and try to get into us.

We knew that we were one of the best passing sides in the league at the time, so we knew that we would have a lot of the ball.

In the end, we had *more* than a lot of the ball that day!

We travelled up to London the night before and stayed in a hotel, before driving to the stadium the next day.

We had been to Wembley a few years before for the Championship Play-Off Final in 2011. That day was scarier than the cup final – there were more nerves before that one.

This is because everything was on the line in that game. We had the chance to go into one of the biggest leagues in the world, which is a complete change of lifestyle, so there was more riding on the win.

Being at Wembley again for the League Cup was different. There were slightly less fans than the previous time, but it is always a great occasion to go to Wembley and we were looking forward to it.

It was a freezing night as we walked out into the stadium, but I can cope with that. As a player, it's better to be too cold than too hot as you can just die of exhaustion when it's like that. Being cold you can get warm, and once you've warmed up and you're out on the pitch you don't necessarily feel it.

It's a great pitch to play on – it's Wembley, so it had to be top notch. It had been watered before the match, which – combined with the bigger size of the field – suited our passing game more so than Bradford.

Of course, the main thing I remember about the first half was scoring the opening goal of the game in the 16th minute.

We had an attack down the centre with Wayne taking it toward the goal, before passing out to Michu, who took a shot. I was always told to take a gamble at the back post, so I kept on running. The keeper saved Michu's shot, but the rebound fell loose, leaving me with a nice little tap-in.

Nothing too big, but a goal is a goal and it felt amazing to score at Wembley.

Some strikers will have their own celebrations that they always do after a goal, but when you don't score all the time, you just let your emotions take you to wherever they take you.

For my first goal I turned my shirt around so my name was on the front so that everyone could see, and I ran off all the way down the line to the other end of the stadium to celebrate with our fans.

Being first on the scoresheet in such a big game was a great highlight for me. That set us up to win the game comfortably.

Michu scored our second in the 40th minute by sliding one to the far post. It was a good goal, but it wasn't the best that day – my second goal takes that honour!

It was 2-0 at half-time and it had been very easy for us, almost like an attack v defence training session.

We thought that Bradford were going to come out and start smashing us, like they really should have done. Had they tried to mess up our flow it may have been a different story, but they sat back.

When teams do that it becomes very easy for us, as we can pass it forever, as we would do in training.

Bradford were deflated after we had scored the second and we could see the life had gone from them. When you see that, you just pounce on it.

Despite the one-sided game, I never felt sorry for them in any way. We were there to win, they were there to win, so you can't start feeling any sympathy for them, regardless of the score.

We didn't have to change anything at half-time and Michael just said, 'Keep doing what you're doing.' Which is exactly what we did as we put our third past them two minutes into the second half.

It was a counter attack – I travelled down the right side and put a ball in. Michu dummied it and it went to Wayne, who played a one-two back to me. I cut inside on my left foot and just curled it to the far corner.

It was a very good goal and exactly the kind of thing we would work on in training. *That* was the best goal of the day. But because we were 3-0 up, it was less of an intense celebration than my first.

Then, when the clock reached 55 minutes, Jonathan de Guzman was taken down in their box by their keeper and we were given a penalty.

Now, I was on my hat-trick and – had I scored another goal – I would have been the first player in history to score a hat-trick in the League Cup Final. So I wanted to take it. But Jonathan wouldn't hand over the ball.

We didn't have a designated penalty taker at the time. If anyone was going to take it, it would have been Michu, but even he was telling Jonathan to give the ball to me.

It was just a bit of an argument back and forth, but he had the ball and I wasn't going to wrestle him for it. He either gave it to me or he didn't.

Of course, he didn't, because he said he wanted to score a goal in a cup final. Eventually, he ended up scoring two.

It's not in my nature to argue like that and it wasn't until somebody said, 'Nath, you take the penalty and get a hat-trick,' that I really wanted to.

I've not taken many penalties in my career – certainly not in the Premier League era – but I would have happily stood up and taken one that day.

If it was the other way around, I would have definitely handed over the ball, but that was that. If he had missed, everyone would have said he was selfish and should have given the ball to me. But he scored and we were ahead, 4-0.

At that moment in time I felt devastated but we made up as soon as he scored. We were cruising to victory, so it didn't bother me too much.

After that though, everyone was passing me the ball, trying to help me get my hat-trick. By that stage I was tired and they kept passing to me in the wrong moments, just because they wanted me to score so badly. But it wasn't going to happen.

I was subbed with ten minutes to go. I have no idea why – it could have been tactical or it could have been to allow somebody else to have their experience in a cup final. I was fine with that, as I had done my part and scored two important goals.

Jonathan scored our final goal in the 91st minute to take us to 5-0, as I watched on from the bench. Moments later it was all over.

It was such a buzz to hear the final whistle confirming that we had won the cup. Some of our players had never been to Wembley before and winning there would have been the highlight of their careers. To look back and say you were a part of that is just brilliant.

There was less raw emotion compared to when we had won the play-off final, because – as I mentioned – that was the £90m game and was career-changing. That game against Reading, we were 3-0 up at half-time, then they came back to 3-2, and there was a lot of pressure to hold on.

This game was a bit more relaxed and controlled by us, so it was more of an expected win.

It may have been more exciting if it was a tighter game, but we were happy with a comfortable win – I think everyone would agree! It was nice for us to just enjoy ourselves on the pitch and that's exactly what we did for that game.

The icing on the cake was being named man of the match. I can't pinpoint exactly why I was given it, but that season was one of the best for me as a footballer and I was playing really well. I had lots of confidence and was doing the job on the pitch.

To be a good winger these days is different. Back in the day, it was about getting past your man and getting a cross in – maybe popping up with a few goals now and again.

It's changed now and these days there's more focus on coming inside, playing through-balls and making runs over the top of defenders. It's changed over the years and it will keep changing as the game develops.

The celebrations in the dressing room after the match were exactly what you would imagine, with singing and champagne spraying everywhere, although I believe that was the time I was called to do a random drugs test, so I missed quite a lot of it.

I was just locked in a room by myself for a while, but I eventually rejoined everyone for a good celebration. This mainly consisted of getting very drunk. When we returned to Swansea, we had a private party put on for us as a team, which allowed us to let our hair down and enjoy the moment.

Of course, we were guaranteed European football the following season because of the win. Playing in Europe was another situation where we could go and have fun – go see what we could do and see how far we could go.

It was a nice bonus, but everything I've experienced in my career feels like a bonus.

To play a certain amount of games in the Premier League is one thing, then to win cups and play in Europe is another. Not many people can say they've played in Europe against some unbelievable teams.

Winning the League Cup and making history for Swansea is a highlight of my career.

A few seasons later, when I was on loan at Leicester, I helped make history for them too. That season was mental but winning the league with them was a different kind of buzz.

I didn't start all of the games, I was coming on from the bench quite a bit, but I was still a part of the team that won the Premier League. As I said, it's a different feeling to the things I have done at Swansea, but unbelievable nonetheless.

Overall, my career with Swansea has been amazing and I've had a great time playing here.

I came here in 2009 and, to play the kind of football that we did at the start, was a dream come true.

Going on to play as many games as I have, and to be part of the history that we have created at Swansea – and to have my name remembered as somebody who was involved in it – is just amazing.

LEON BRITTON: BORN 16 SEPTEMBER 1982, MERTON; 463 GAMES, 11 GOALS

Leon Britton

Swansea City 3-0 Cardiff City
Premier League
Liberty Stadium, 8 February 2014

When it comes to Swansea City legends, it's hard to top Leon Britton in terms of longevity, consistency, and club pride. Since his arrival in December 2002, the compact midfielder has been a constant force in the centre of the pitch, spanning 16 seasons and more than ten different managers. While he started as a winger, he moved into midfield under Roberto Martinez and quickly became the catalyst for all things good in a passing-focused team. In fact, in 2012, he was statistically the top passer in European football. Britton has represented Swansea in all four tiers of the league, and featured in countless iconic games for the club including Hull 2003, Carlisle 2006, Reading 2011, Bradford 2013, and – as he discusses in this chapter – Cardiff 2014.

Swansea City: Vorm, Rangel, Davies, Williams, Chico, Britton, Dyer (Taylor), de Guzman (Canas), Bony, Emnes (Hernandez), Routledge

Cardiff City: Marshall, Fabio (McNaughton), John, Medel, Caulker, Turner, Bellamy, Whittingham, Jones (Campbell), Kim, Zaha (Mutch)

Swansea Scorers: Routledge, Dyer, Bony

Referee: A. Marriner

Attendance: 20,402

HAVING enjoyed such a lengthy career with Swansea City, I've been fortunate to play in many South Wales derby matches. Some have been brilliant – some, not so great.

One of my favourites was the game we played against Cardiff in the League Cup in September 2008, mainly because the clubs hadn't played each other for so long. About nine years I think.

We had always just missed them. We had been in League 2 when Cardiff were in League 1, then when we were promoted to League 1, Cardiff went up to the Championship. We were always a little bit behind them in those days.

In 2008 it was our first season in the Championship, so we were due to play them twice anyway, but the League Cup threw us together first.

The build-up for that one was so intense. You could really feel the tension mounting around the city – everyone was waiting for that match.

A lot of the Cardiff matches would tend to be early kick-offs to keep the crowds under control, but that one was a rare evening kick-off.

Because it was a night game, I decided to go for lunch in town around one or two o'clock in the afternoon.

Even at that time, people were already in the pubs and bars. That was my first derby game so, at first, I wasn't sure what to expect. But after seeing that, I knew, 'This is something different.'

It eventually ended in a 1-0 win for us, with Jordi Gomez scoring from a free kick. He hit it under the wall, it came off the studs of one of their players, and skidded into the top corner. Fantastic.

Then, in November 2009, we won 3-2 at home under Paulo Sousa, which was another very good game. Nathan Dyer scored a header, Darren Pratley scored a scissor-kick, and then he scored the winner with an amazing volley from Fede Bessone's cross.

I didn't play in the derby at Cardiff City Stadium when we won 1-0 in 2010 – the one where Marvin Emnes scored late on. I was with Sheffield United at that point and I watched the match on telly, which was a bit of a strange experience.

Winning was always an amazing feeling. Mind you, we lost a few too.

At the Liberty Stadium in 2011, I remember Craig Bellamy scored a brilliant goal to win it for them. It was 0-0 and not much was happening, until he produced a top-class strike from 30 yards out with five minutes to go.

Another horrible one was up at Cardiff City Stadium in 2010. We were 1-0 up after Andrea Orlandi took a corner and it went straight in. But then Cardiff came back and Michael Chopra scored two goals – one in the first half, and then the winner in injury time. We lost the game 2-1. That was pretty sickening, conceding so late.

But the hardest one for me to take was the final game at Ninian Park in April 2009. It was 1-1 for most of the game before Joe Allen – who was only a young lad back then – scored a brilliant goal for us late on. However, as it got to the final minute of the match, Mike Dean – who had been hit by a coin earlier in that game – gave the softest penalty to Cardiff.

He knew what was riding on the game and, in my opinion, he bottled it.

Being the last one at Ninian Park, it would have been a great match for Swansea to win, but the ref made a bad decision and we ended up sharing the points.

This leads me on to one of the more recent games against Cardiff, and the season where one of my favourite games in a Swans shirt took place.

As we reached the middle of the 2013/14 season, things weren't going well for us. We were in a poor run of form, and we had dropped down the table to the point that we were involved in a relegation battle.

It was our third season in the Premier League. The two seasons before had been so enjoyable and successful, but we were playing badly and started to fall away.

A relegation battle was looming, which was something different for us as a football club and for a lot of us as players.

We knew we had to pick things up, otherwise we were in real danger of dropping out of the league.

It's hard to pinpoint exactly why things had become so bad, especially because we had a talented squad made up of pretty much the same players as the year before.

I think being in the Europa League had something to do with it. It was tough playing on Thursday nights then again on Sundays, and it started taking its toll on the squad.

That period ended with Michael Laudrup being sacked at the start of February.

It's disappointing when any manager gets the sack because, ultimately, it's the players who have underperformed.

We all take responsibility – the managers, the staff and the players – but it's the players who cross the white line on matchdays, so it's largely down to us.

It was especially disappointing to learn Michael had gone. We played some brilliant football under him and won our first major trophy in the League Cup Final. It was really enjoyable for the players, and for the fans to watch.

But that's football.

If the team isn't getting the results, the pressure mounts and there's a lot of speculation. That's why sometimes it's not the biggest surprise when the manager goes.

We were disappointed for Michael and his staff, but we had to remain professional and concentrated on moving forward.

Of course, his replacement was Garry Monk.

I was chuffed for Garry, because I had played with him for many years and knew that management was a route he wanted to go down.

It was a big opportunity for him, but it was also a big task coming in and taking on a Premier League team that was struggling as we were.

We had shared a changing room with him only one week before and suddenly he was caretaker manager, so the players were all behind him. I was good friends with him – I still am – and I spoke to him when he got the job. I told him that we were there for him and if he needed help or feedback, we would give it.

Garry was club captain for many years, and he was always a leader and fit for the role. Reliable, consistent, professional – those are the words you put next to Garry's name. So, as difficult as it might have been for him, I think the transition into management was quite natural.

His first game in charge happened to be one of the most important of the season – the South Wales derby.

We'd taken on Cardiff earlier in the season, in November at the Cardiff City Stadium. As we expected, there was a big build-up to that one.

There's always hype going into derby games, but that one in particular was very big as it was the first South Wales derby in the Premier League and it was on telly, broadcast around the world.

The actual game itself wasn't the greatest and we lost 1-0. Steven Caulker scored the goal, which was difficult – it always is when a former player scores against you.

We knew what was expected of us that day, but we were poor and we can't argue with the result. We didn't perform and we didn't deserve to win, it's as simple as that.

From a player's point of view, the South Wales derby isn't something you really look forward to, because of the bigger build-up and pressure to not lose the game.

Of course, you don't want to lose any game you play, but going into those games you know what's riding on it for your supporters and your city.

The rivalry between Swansea and Cardiff is deep but having been here for so many years I've come to realise that it's not just football related.

I think there's more resentment from Swansea towards Cardiff. I'm not fully qualified to explain the situation because I don't know the ins and outs, but the sense I get is that Cardiff gets all the government funding and backing, and Swansea is left behind a bit.

So, it's a cultural thing as well, although that takes nothing away from the intense footballing rivalry.

There's big pressure going into a derby match anyway, but it was even worse because we knew that neither team had done the league double over the other in one season before. That was something that had been talked about a lot in the build-up.

It was also something we really wanted to avoid as players.

As Cardiff had already won the first game, you don't want to be part of a Swansea team that suffers two derby defeats in one season. That plays on your mind quite a bit because you just don't want your name attached to that record.

After a big build-up in the media, the day finally arrived on 8 February – a miserable winter's evening, just four days after Garry was appointed to his new role.

For home games my preparation is always the same, and it was no different for the Cardiff match.

I wake up in the morning, drive down to the shop to buy a couple of bottles of Lucozade, come back and make scrambled eggs and beans on toast, get changed, then make my way to the stadium.

Usually we'll get to the stadium quite early – before the fans start to arrive. But for a derby game I find when approaching the stadium there are a lot more supporters already around the ground.

We normally have our pre-match meal three hours before kick-off. So, if it's a 3pm kick-off, we'll meet around 11.45am, then have our meal at midday, then have a team meeting around 1pm.

That meeting is where the manager – Garry in this instance – runs through the last few things he wants us to do in the match. Then it's down to the changing rooms, where we get ready and switch on.

I can't remember exactly what Garry's pre-match team talk went like, but he made sure everyone was aware how much the game meant to the supporters and the city, and that we should remain professional and keep our emotions in check.

That's one of the key things in derby games – use the energy of the fans, but don't get too carried away by emotions and end up doing something out of character.

That night he put out an attacking team. Fair play to Garry for his selections and for going bold when he could have been defensive.

Especially with the situation we were in. Having been in bad form and struggling, it would have been easy for him to try to keep things tight then opened up as the game went on. But the line-up that night was brave.

It would have been a 4-2-3-1, with myself and Jonathan de Guzman in midfield, Nathan on the right, Wayne on the left, with Marvin as a 10 just behind Wilfried. Those are all attacking players – even de Guzman, who was next to me in midfield, was a pretty attacking player.

Walking out into the stadium, the atmosphere was incredible. On derby days it really is a special atmosphere. It builds up from the moment we go out for our warm-up, but as we finally walk down the tunnel and on to the pitch, it's a ferocious noise level that's a couple of notches above normal games.

It was hammering down with rain that night. I think that can help Swansea because of the passing game we play – when there's water on the pitch the ball moves a bit quicker. Playing on a dry pitch is always harder as the ball sticks and doesn't move as quickly, giving the opposition time to get back in shape.

I actually can't remember much of the first half, in terms of action. I know it was quite tight and both sides had decent chances. Either us or Cardiff realistically could have been in front after the first 45 minutes, but we ended up walking in to the changing rooms goalless.

It was the second half where things really came to life, especially as, two minutes into the second half, we went ahead.

Pablo Hernandez had come on for Marvin at half-time, and he had the ball in the left side of their half. Wayne was playing left wing and made a run behind their full-back when Pablo played a perfectly weighted pass to him.

Despite the slickness of the pitch, he timed that pass perfectly. He had the quality to find the killer final pass and that one was right up there – possibly the best pass he made in his Swansea career.

It was a clever run from Wayne too, who collected the ball and put a confident finish past David Marshall. A great goal against his old team, as he had been on loan at Cardiff a few years before.

It was the 78th minute when Nathan made it 2-0. I think it was Wayne who crossed it in from the left. Nath darted in between the full-back and centre-back, dived and headed it into the far corner. It was a great diving header from the smallest man on the pitch.

Over the years we've always had banter over who's smaller – me or him. Sometimes he'll grow his hair a bit to gain a few extra inches, but that doesn't count.

If someone visits the training ground, we'll sometimes stand next to each other and ask them to judge. But there's never a definitive answer. Sometimes someone will say I'm taller, the next person will say it's Nath.

It's a close one, but he's *definitely* smaller than me.

Nath's not known for his heading due to his size, but I'm sure he scored with his head against Cardiff at the Liberty in 2009. Maybe it's something about Cardiff that brings out the best of his heading ability!

Despite the banter we have, I've never looked at size as an issue.

Of course, there are some disadvantages – someone who is 6ft 3in is going to win a header over me. I'll compete, but the law of averages means I'm going to lose more often than not. But there are also advantages. Being smaller means that I have a low centre of gravity, I can turn a lot quicker, and manipulate the ball a lot better because I am closer to it.

Growing up I was always a midfielder, but at West Ham they pushed me out to the wing, maybe because they didn't think I was physical enough.

The same happened at Swansea – I played on the right wing under Kenny Jackett, because he wanted to go with a more physical midfield.

It was Roberto who changed it, bringing me into the centre of midfield. From that moment I learned the holding midfield role, and just tried to perfect it. I was a good technical player, made sure I always read the game well, and also ensured my short passing was accurate.

In fact, in 2012, it was quite well documented that I was statistically the top passer in Europe.

We had been in the Championship where the spotlight isn't quite as big as the Premier League, but when we were promoted all these stats are suddenly thrown at us. And that was one of them.

The thing is, my game is very safe. I'm not one for longer passing and taking lots of risks, so my pass completion was always going to be quite high.

Still, to finish top was quite strange, especially to see my name alongside Xavi, Busquets, and those kinds of players.

But I took it with a pinch of salt and I didn't get carried away. I got a little bit of stick from the others, but that's normal!

Back to the Cardiff game and it was Wilf who finished the night in style. Of all the goals that night, it's the one I remember the best.

It was a good out-swinging free kick taken by Pablo near the corner, which met the head of Wilf as he leapt. He was just so strong and put it into the far corner. I think it clipped the crossbar on the way in, but it was a great goal with about five minutes left. Game over.

That season in particular, Wilf's goals were so important.

He was a great goalscorer, but there's more to him than just putting the ball in the back of the net. Wilf is very much a leader. He's very vocal in the changing room before the game, at half-time, and during the game.

He's a big presence for the team. Attacking-wise he's very strong and holds the ball up for us. You can get the ball up to him and know he's going to hold it. Especially when the pressure is on, like when we're playing away and the home team are pressing us.

I know we can get the ball to Wilf and it'll stick, allowing us to get up the pitch a bit. That was one of his biggest strengths.

Defensively too, he's very important for us. He's very good in the air, which is crucial for defending corners, for example.

Over the years we'll have told players to man-mark specific people, but with Wilfried we just say, 'Wilf, stay in the middle and wherever that ball goes, you go and attack it.'

That night, he had made a big impact against Cardiff, basically sealing the win for us.

After that goal went in and it was 3-0, I could relax. When it's 1-0 or 2-0, it's still a bit cagey because the game can change in a split second. But when it's 3-0 – and it was quite late on – you feel it is job done.

You can start to enjoy the atmosphere and take it in a little bit. It's normally hard to take in the occasion in those games, as they are usually so tight, but that was the biggest margin I've had against Cardiff.

When the final whistle went, we were buzzing, but there was also a feeling of relief.

Of course, you savour the moment – as I'm sure the Cardiff players would have when they won – but because of the pressure that was there in the build-up, relief was just as big an emotion that night.

At the end of the day it was still a league match, but you can't deny it's a different game to the others. If we beat Cardiff it's going to be a different set of emotions for the players and the fans compared to if we'd beat, say, Southampton the week before.

Everyone is in great spirits afterwards. I love mixing with the fans after a derby win, because they are on cloud nine. They'll come up and tell me that they've got a Cardiff friend they work with, or a mate who supports Cardiff, and they tell you how they're going to give them some stick next week.

Most importantly, that result really kick-started our season because of the confidence it gave us.

Having Garry – a club legend – win a game immediately after taking the position of caretaker manager instantly lifted the club and the supporters. For that win to come against our biggest rivals just lifted everyone even higher.

From then until the end of the season we went on a decent run, picked up some points, and finished the season pretty strongly.

There are certain moments that have an effect on the season for good or for bad, and that Cardiff game was a game-changer in terms of the upturn of confidence and belief we gained.

I've been with Swansea for 16 seasons and many individual moments stand out. For me though, my first season with the club, coming down on loan from West Ham, was one of my favourites.

I know it was League 2 and we didn't play at the kind of grounds we play at now or in front of those big crowds, but I always look back on that year fondly.

It was my first year in professional football, playing with a good bunch of lads. We had great team spirit and we went on to become very good friends.

Of course, things weren't going well for Swansea at the time. The club was bottom of the league, struggling to survive, and it all came down to the Hull game at the Vetch.

It was just brilliant – but only because we won and stayed in the league. Overall, that first season for me as a professional still takes some beating.

There's others, like the 2010/11 season when we were promoted to the Premier League, which was a dream come true for so many of us. A lot of us had been together in that team for a long time, working up through the leagues, which made it all the more special.

My aim – having joined Swansea from a Premier League team – was always to get back playing in the top flight. To do it with Swansea, at Wembley, in front of 40,000 Swansea fans, was just unbelievable.

I know I missed the first six months when I was up at Sheffield United, but that season was huge. The football we were playing under Brendan was great, and some of the games it produced made it hard to beat.

I'll never forget the play-off semi-final, when I scored against Forest.

I don't score many goals, but that will always be my favourite, because it was the best goal I scored in a technical sense, as well as what was riding on the game.

Of course, when I signed my first professional contract at Swansea in 2003, I'd never have dreamed I would be here in 2018, after 15 years. Never. Neither could I have dreamed of the journey it has been.

When I first joined Swansea, I was on trial for two weeks. Brian Flynn said, 'Come down – you look at us, we'll look at you, and we'll go from there.'

But I ended up signing a month's loan, which turned into six months.

As I said, my original plan when I first came down was to do well at Swansea, then go back to West Ham to try to push through into their first team. But at the end of the season – after we had beaten Hull – West Ham told me that I was free to leave, even though I had a year left on my contract.

I could have tried to find a team in the division above, but I had enjoyed it so much at Swansea I didn't have to speak with any other clubs. Swansea gave me the opportunity when nobody else would.

In reality, I could have spent 15 years in League 2 with Swansea, but the way things have developed – going all the way through the leagues then establishing ourselves in the Premier League – has been so special.

I don't think anyone could have predicted it. I'm not just talking about my career, but the way Swansea have grown from where we were when I joined, to the club we are now.

It's been a privilege to have been here for so long, and to have been a part of so many memorable Swansea games. To be able to say 'I was part of that' just gives me great pride.

Three promotions, establishing ourselves in the Premier League, a League Cup win, European football, beating some of the biggest teams in the world; it's a dream scenario. I couldn't have asked for better.

One of the things that has made it such a memorable career is the Swansea fans. From day one, I've always found the fans great. I remember making my debut against Exeter in December 2002. I think we took maybe 1,000 fans there because, believe it or not, that was one of the closer grounds for us!

I remember making a couple of tackles quite early on in the game, and I remember them instantly chanting my name – 'Leon, Leon!'

The backing that they've given me has really been outstanding. Sometimes they've given me so much confidence because I know I've got their support.

Whether that was jumping up from League 2 to League 1 and questioning whether I was good enough, or simply having a bad game, they stand behind you regardless.

One weird thing that stands out is when I was a Sheffield United player, Swansea played Wigan in the League Cup and I went along to the game at the DW Stadium.

I was actually a bit apprehensive about going, because I had only just left the Swans. I didn't know what reaction I would get off the fans.

But when I got there it was incredible.

Everyone was singing my name in the stands. That was perhaps one of my favourite moments in my career, even though I wasn't playing with Swansea at the time.

Then, coming back, they showed me the same support they had shown me in previous years.

The fans and the people of Swansea have been great, and I owe them so much for where I am today.